175 Vegetarian Salads

175 Vegetarian Salads

Make tempting salads, dressings and dips all year round with easy-to-follow recipes and 180 photographs

Julia Canning

southwater

This edition is published by Southwater Books, an imprint of Anness Publishing Ltd, Hermes House, 88–89 Blackfriars Road, London SE1 8HA; tel. 020 7401 2077; fax 020 7633 9499
www.southwater.co.uk; www.annesspublishing.com

If you like the images in this book and would like to investigate using them for publishing, promotions or advertising, please visit our website www.practicalpictures.com for more information.

UK agent: The Manning Partnership Ltd; tel. 01225 478444; fax 01225 478440; sales@manning-partnership.co.uk

UK distributor: Grantham Book Services Ltd; tel. 01476 541080; fax 01476 541061; orders@gbs.tbs-ltd.co.uk

North American agent/distributor: National Book Network; tel. 301 459 3366; fax 301 429 5746; www.nbnbooks.com

Australian agent/distributor: Pan Macmillan Australia; tel. 1300 135 113; fax 1300 135 103; customer.service@macmillan.com.au

New Zealand agent/distributor: David Bateman Ltd; tel. (09) 415 7664; fax (09) 415 8892

ETHICAL TRADING POLICY
At Anness Publishing we believe that business should be conducted in an ethical and ecologically sustainable way, with respect for the environment and a proper regard to the replacement of the natural resources we employ. As a publisher, we use a lot of wood pulp to make high-quality paper for printing, and that wood commonly comes from spruce trees. We are therefore currently growing more than 750,000 trees in three Scottish forest plantations: Berrymoss (130 hectares/320 acres), West Touxhill (125 hectares/305 acres) and Deveron Forest (75 hectares/185 acres). The forests we manage contain more than 3.5 times the number of trees employed each year in making paper for the books we manufacture.

Because of this ongoing ecological investment programme, you, as our customer, can have the pleasure and reassurance of knowing that a tree is being cultivated on your behalf to naturally replace the materials used to make the book you are holding.

Our forestry programme is run in accordance with the UK Woodland Assurance Scheme (UKWAS) and will be certified by the internationally recognized Forest Stewardship Council (FSC). The FSC is a non-government organization dedicated to promoting responsible management of the world's forests. Certification ensures forests are managed in an environmentally sustainable and socially responsible way. For further information about this scheme, go to www.annesspublishing.com/trees

Previously published as part of a larger volume, *500 Sensational Salads.*

Publisher: Joanna Lorenz
Project Editor: Kate Eddison
Jacket Design: Nigel Partridge
Production Controller: Pirong Wang

Notes
Bracketed terms are intended for American readers.

For all recipes, quantities are given in both metric and imperial measures and, where appropriate, in standard cups and spoons. Follow one set of measures, but not a mixture, because they are not interchangeable.

Standard spoon and cup measures are level.
1 tsp = 5ml, 1 tbsp = 15ml, 1 cup = 250ml/8fl oz

Australian standard tablespoons are 20ml. Australian readers should use 3 tsp in place of 1 tbsp for measuring small quantities.

American pints are 16fl oz/2 cups. American readers should use 20fl oz/2.5 cups in place of 1 pint when measuring liquids.

Electric oven temperatures in this book are for conventional ovens. When using a fan oven, the temperature will probably need to be reduced by about 10–20°C/20–40°F. Since ovens vary, you should check with your manufacturer's instruction book for guidance.

The nutritional analysis given for each recipe is calculated per portion (i.e. serving or item), unless otherwise stated. If the recipe gives a range, such as Serves 4–6, then the nutritional analysis will be for the smaller portion size, i.e. 6 servings. Measurements for sodium do not include salt added to taste.

Medium (US large) eggs are used unless otherwise stated.

Main front cover image shows Roasted Vegetable Pasta Salad – for recipe, see page 67.

Although the advice and information in this book are believed to be accurate and true at the time of going to press, neither the authors nor the publisher can accept any legal responsibility or liability for any errors or omissions that may be made.

Contents

Introduction

Salads are the perfect choice for contemporary meals. Quick, easy and composed of the freshest ingredients, they provide the healthy answer to the eternal question of what to serve for lunch or supper. There's a salad here for every occasion, from snacks through light lunches to casual suppers and formal dinners, demonstrating the variety of fresh and colourful vegetarian dishes. You will find simple dressings and dips, appetizers and substantial main meal salads based on vegetables, eggs and cheese, beans and lentils, and rice, grains, pasta and noodles. There is also a delicious selection of fruit salads, which make great desserts but are also ideal for light breakfasts.

Because salads are usually based on fresh produce, they are more ingredient-driven than other dishes. It is no use planning to serve a superb salad, only to discover that the central ingredient is out of season, or looks limp and unappetizing after a long journey from some foreign field. It makes sense, therefore, to abandon the usual practice of basing a meal around specific recipes before going shopping. Instead, check out what's freshest and best, and then plan your menu. Farm shops and farmers' markets are a great source of seasonal vegetables and fruits, or you may belong to a box scheme, and have a regular delivery of freshly pulled or picked produce. You may even grow your own – seed suppliers increasingly offer packs that are perfect for growing in pots.

Every country has its own favourite salad and it is fascinating to see how many ways there are of presenting the same ingredient. Take something as simple as a tomato, for instance. In Italy it might be sliced with mozzarella cheese and basil to make a tricolore salad, while in Turkey and Greece, feta cheese and black olives are popular additions. A favourite Mexican treatment is to use tomatoes in all sorts of salsas, sometimes with the chillies that are so common in that

country, but also with oranges and chives, coriander (cilantro) or other fresh herbs. Tomato salads can also include grains, for example couscous or bulgur wheat, and are great blended with carbohydrate-rich pasta or rice, turning them into a substantial meal.

Meat-free salads can make substantial meals with a variety of nutritious additions, from beans, lentils, eggs and cheese to rice, grains, pasta and noodles. Try Warm Dressed Salad with Poached Eggs, Spanish Rice Salad or Roasted Vegetable Pasta Salad. More unusual offerings include Roquefort and Flageolet Bean Salad with Honey Dressing, Tabbouleh with Tomatoes and Apricots, and Fruit and Raw Vegetable Gado-gado.

The golden rule when making a salad is to choose just a few ingredients with complementary or contrasting textures and compatible flavours. Vegetables or fruits will provide plenty of colour, but you can also add edible flowers such as nasturtiums, marigolds or borage to enliven green leaves. Use herbs with discretion: rocket gives green salads a lovely peppery flavour, but tastes best when balanced with milder green leaves or with a sweet fruit such as pears or figs. Parsley, dill, mint and basil all make good additions when matched with other flavours.

Salad servers can be used for mixing, but many cooks prefer to use clean hands, since they are softer and less likely to bruise delicate leaves. Use only enough dressing to gloss the ingredients, enhancing their flavour without being too dominant. It is usual to add salad dressing just before serving, but some recipes require a little time to marinate. The salads in this book come with carefully selected dressings, but by mixing and matching, you can create your own combinations.

Choosing salad dressings can be a tricky decision for a vegetarian. Store-bought dressings often contain hidden non-vegetarian ingredients, such as Worcestershire sauce. The dressings and dips in this book will allow you to rest assured that you know exactly what went into them.

This book is beautifully illustrated with 180 photographs, showing the finished dishes. All of the salads have been analysed by a nutritionist, and the energy, carbohydrate, fat, protein, fibre, calcium and sodium are detailed under each entry to enable you to plan delicious and nutritious meals.

Saffron Dip

Serve this mild dip with crudités – it's especially good with cauliflower.

Makes about 220ml/ 7½fl oz/1 cup

15ml/1 tbsp boiling water
small pinch of saffron threads
200g/7oz/scant 1 cup fromage frais
10 fresh chives
10 fresh basil leaves
5ml/1 tsp paprika
salt and ground black pepper

1 Infuse the saffron strands in the freshly boiled water for 3 minutes.

2 Beat the fromage frais until smooth and soft, then stir in the saffron infusion.

3 Using scissors, snip the chives into the dip. Tear the basil leaves into small pieces and stir them in.

4 Season with salt and freshly ground black pepper to taste and serve immediately.

French Dressing

French vinaigrette is one of the most widely used salad dressings in the world.

Makes about 120ml/ 4fl oz/½ cup

90ml/6 tbsp extra virgin olive oil
15ml/1 tbsp white wine vinegar
5ml/1 tsp French mustard
pinch of caster (superfine) sugar

1 Place the extra virgin olive oil and white wine vinegar in a clean screw-top jar.

2 Add the French mustard and caster sugar.

3 Replace the lid and shake well until all the ingredients are thoroughly combined.

Creamy Raspberry Dressing

This tangy dressing goes very well with asparagus instead of hollandaise sauce.

Makes about 100ml/ 3fl oz/⅓ cup

30ml/2 tbsp raspberry vinegar
2.5ml/½ tsp salt
5ml/1 tsp Dijon mustard
60ml/4 tbsp crème fraîche or natural (plain) yogurt
ground white pepper

1 Mix the vinegar and salt in a bowl and stir with a fork until the salt is dissolved.

2 Stir in the mustard, crème fraîche or yogurt and add pepper to taste.

French Herb Dressing

The delicate scents and flavours of fresh herbs combine especially well in a French dressing. Use just one herb or try a selection. Toss this dressing with a simple green salad and serve with good cheese, fresh bread and wine.

Makes about 120ml/ 4fl oz/½ cup

60ml/4 tbsp extra virgin olive oil
30ml/2 tbsp groundnut (peanut) or sunflower oil
15ml/1 tbsp lemon juice
60ml/4 tbsp finely chopped fresh herbs
pinch of caster (superfine) sugar

1 Place the olive oil and groundnut or sunflower oil in a clean screw-top jar.

2 Add the lemon juice, finely chopped fresh herbs and caster sugar.

3 Replace the lid and shake well until all the ingredients are thoroughly combined.

Thousand Island Dressing

This creamy dressing is great with green salads and grated carrot, hot potato, pasta and rice salads.

Makes about 120ml/ 4fl oz/½ cup

60ml/4 tbsp sunflower oil
15ml/1 tbsp orange juice
15ml/1 tbsp lemon juice
10ml/2 tsp grated lemon rind
15ml/1 tbsp finely chopped onion
5ml/1 tsp paprika
5ml/1 tsp vegetarian Worcestershire sauce
15ml/1 tbsp finely chopped fresh parsley
salt and ground black pepper

1 Put the oil, orange juice, lemon juice, lemon rind, onion, paprika, vegetarian Worcestershire sauce and parsley into a screw-top jar.

2 Season to taste with salt and ground black pepper.

3 Replace the lid and shake well until all the ingredients are thoroughly combined.

Blue Cheese & Chive Dressing

Blue cheese dressings have a strong, robust flavour and are well suited to winter salad leaves such as escarole, chicory and radicchio.

Makes about 350ml/ 12fl oz/1½ cups

75g/3oz blue cheese (Stilton, Bleu d'Auvergne or Gorgonzola)
150ml/¼ pint/⅔ cup natural (plain) yogurt
45ml/3 tbsp olive oil
30ml/2 tbsp lemon juice
15ml/1 tbsp chopped fresh chives
ground black pepper

1 Remove the rind from the cheese and combine with a third of the yogurt in a bowl.

2 Add the remainder of the yogurt, the olive oil and the lemon juice.

3 Stir in the chopped chives and season to taste with ground black pepper.

Coriander Dressing & Marinade

This simple dressing has a pleasing bite, and works well as a dressing for leaves or as a marinade for tofu.

Makes about 475ml/ 16fl oz/2 cups

120ml/4floz/½ cup lemon juice
30ml/2 tbsp wholegrain mustard
250ml/8fl oz/1 cup olive oil
75ml/5 tbsp sesame oil
5ml/1 tsp coriander seeds, crushed

1 Mix all the ingredients together in a bowl. Chill the dressing until you are ready to serve.

2 If desired, pour over tofu pieces and leave, covered, in the refrigerator overnight, until you are ready to cook them.

Yogurt Dressing

This dressing is a less rich version of a classic mayonnaise. It is much quicker and easier to make, too.

Makes about 210ml/ 7fl oz/scant 1 cup

150 ml/¼ pint/⅔ cup natural (plain) yogurt
30ml/2 tbsp mayonnaise
30ml/2 tbsp milk
15ml/1 tbsp chopped fresh parsley
15ml/1 tbsp chopped fresh chives
salt and ground black pepper

1 Put all the ingredients together in a bowl.

2 Season to taste and mix well.

Mayonnaise

For consistent results, ensure that both egg yolks and oil are at room temperature before combining. Home-made mayonnaise is made with raw egg yolks and may be considered unsuitable for young children, pregnant mothers and the elderly.

Makes about 300 ml/ ½ pint/1¼ cups

2 egg yolks
5ml/1 tsp French mustard
150ml/¼ pint/⅔ cup extra virgin olive oil
150ml/¼ pint/⅔ cup groundnut or sunflower oil
10ml/2 tsp white wine vinegar
salt and ground black pepper

1 Place the egg yolks and mustard in a food processor and blend smoothly.

2 Add the olive oil a little at a time while the processor is running.

3 When the mixture is thick, add the groundnut or sunflower oil in a slow, steady stream.

4 Add the vinegar and season to taste with salt and pepper.

Garlic Mayonnaise

Use ready-made mayonnaise to save time, and blanch the garlic in boiling water if you prefer a milder flavour.

Makes about 300 ml/½ pint/1¼ cups

2 egg yolks
5ml/1 tsp French mustard
150ml/¼ pint/⅔ cup extra virgin olive oil
150ml/¼ pint/⅔ cup groundnut or sunflower oil
10ml/2 tsp white wine vinegar (or lemon juice or warm water)
2–4 garlic cloves
salt and ground black pepper

1 First make the mayonnaise as in the recipe above. Then crush the garlic cloves with the blade of a knife and stir it into the mayonnaise.

Basil & Lemon Mayonnaise

This luxurious dressing is flavoured with lemon juice and two types of basil. Serve with all kinds of leafy salads, crudités or coleslaws. It is also good served with baked potatoes or as a delicious dip for French fries. This dressing will keep in an airtight jar for up to a week in the refrigerator.

Makes about 300ml/ ½ pint/1¼ cups
2 large egg yolks
15ml/1 tbsp lemon juice
150ml/¼ pint/⅔ cup extra virgin olive oil
150ml/¼ pint/⅔ cup sunflower oil
4 garlic cloves
handful of fresh green basil
handful of fresh opal basil
salt and ground black pepper

1 Place the egg yolks and lemon juice in a blender or food processor and mix them briefly until lightly blended.

2 In a jug (pitcher), stir together the extra virgin olive oil and the sunflower oil. With the motor running, pour the oil mixture into the food processor very slowly, a drop at a time at first, increasing to a thin drizzle.

3 Once half of the oil has been added, and the dressing has successfully emulsified, the remaining oil can be incorporated more quickly. Continue processing until a thick, creamy mayonnaise has formed.

4 Peel and crush the garlic cloves and add to the mayonnaise.

5 Alternatively, place the peeled cloves on a chopping board and sprinkle with salt, then flatten them with the heel of a heavy-bladed knife and chop the flesh. Flatten the garlic again to make a coarse purée. Add to the mayonnaise.

6 Remove the basil stalks and tear both types of leaves into small pieces. Stir into the mayonnaise.

7 Add salt and pepper to taste, then transfer the mayonnaise to a serving dish. Cover and chill until ready to serve.

Hollandaise Sauce

The classic sauce is perfect for drizzling over warm salads, and is particularly good served with fresh asparagus or artichokes.

Serves 6
¾ cup unsalted butter, cut into pieces
3 egg yolks
15ml/1 tbsp cold water
15–30ml/1–2 tbsp lemon juice
½ tsp salt
cayenne pepper

1 Clarify the butter by melting it in a small pan over a low heat; do not boil. Skim off any foam with a perforated spoon.

2 In a small heavy pan or in the top of a double boiler, combine the egg yolks, water, 15ml/1 tbsp of the lemon juice, salt and pepper, and whisk for 1 minute.

3 Place the pan over a very low heat or place the double boiler top over barely simmering water and whisk constantly until the egg yolk mixture begins to thicken and the whisk leaves tracks on the base of the pan. Remove from heat.

4 Whisk in the clarified butter, drop by drop, until the sauce begins to thicken, then pour it in a little more quickly, making sure that the butter is absorbed before adding any more.

5 When you reach the milky solids at the bottom of the clarified butter, stop pouring. Season to taste with salt and cayenne and a little more lemon juice if wished. If the sauce seems too sharp, add a little more butter.

Cook's Tips
• *The sauce has a similar consistency to mayonnaise. To make it thinner, add 15–30ml/1–2 tbsp single (light) cream.*
• *The sauce will keep for up to 1 week. When ready to use, reheat it gently in a bowl over simmering water, whisking constantly to retain the smooth consistency.*

Thousand Island Dip

A great dip to have with red or green (bell) peppers.

Serves 4

4 sun-dried tomatoes in oil
4 plum tomatoes, or 2 beefsteak tomatoes
60ml/4 tbsp mayonnaise
150g/5oz/⅔ cup mild soft cheese, or marscapone or fromage frais
30ml/2 tbsp tomato purée (paste)
30ml/2 tbsp chopped fresh parsley
1 lemon
Tabasco sauce, to taste
5ml/1 tsp soy sauce
salt and ground black pepper

1 Drain the sun-dried tomatoes on kitchen paper. Chop finely.

2 Cut a cross in the base of each fresh tomato. Plunge into freshly boiled water for 30 seconds. Lift out with slotted spoon and place in a bowl of cold water. Drain, remove the skin, halve the tomatoes and discard the seeds. Chop the flesh finely.

3 Beat the mayonnaise, soft cheese and tomato purée together. Stir in the parsley and sun-dried tomatoes, then the fresh tomatoes. Grate the lemon rind finely and add to the dip. Squeeze the lemon and add some juice and Tabasco sauce to taste, then chill until you are ready to serve.

Hummus

A garlicky chickpea dip, ideal with crudités.

Serves 4

400g/4oz can chickpeas, drained
2 garlic cloves
30ml/2 tbsp tahini paste
60ml/4 tbsp olive oil
juice of 1 lemon
2.5ml/½ tsp cayenne pepper
15ml/1 tbsp sesame seeds
sea salt

1 Rinse the chickpeas and whizz in a food blender or processor with the garlic, tahini and a good pinch of salt until smooth. As you blend, slowly pour in the oil and lemon juice.

2 Stir in the cayenne pepper and salt to taste. Add cold water if the mixure is too thick.

3 Lightly toast the sesame seeds in a non-stick frying pan, then sprinkle them over the finished hummus.

Guacamole

Serve with tortilla chips or crudités.

Serves 4

2 ripe avocados
2 tomatoes, peeled, seeded and chopped
6 spring onions (scallions)
30ml/2 tbsp fresh lime juice
15ml/1 tsbp chopped fresh coriander (cilantro)
salt and ground black pepper
fresh coriander (cilantro) sprigs to garnish

1 Mash the ingredients together with a fork and add salt and pepper to taste. Garnish with sprigs of coriander.

Feta, Roast Pepper & Chilli Dip

This tasty Greek dip is a mouthwatering mixture of tangy feta cheese and spicy roasted peppers and chillies. It is perfect served with toasted pitta bread or simply spread on slices of toast. Sprinkle some finely chopped fresh flat leaf parsley on top, if you like.

Serves 4

1 yellow or green elongated or bell-shaped pepper
1–2 fresh green chillies
200g/7oz feta cheese, cubed
60ml/4 tbsp extra virgin olive oil
juice of 1 lemon
45–60ml/3–4 tbsp milk
ground black pepper
finely chopped fresh flat leaf parsley, to garnish
slices of toast or toasted pitta bread, to serve

1 Scorch the pepper and chillies by threading them on to metal skewers and turning them over a flame or under the grill (broiler), until charred all over.

2 Set the pepper and chillies aside until cool enough to handle.

3 Peel off as much of their skin as possible and wipe off the blackened parts with kitchen paper.

4 Slit the pepper and chillies and discard the seeds and stems.

5 Put the pepper and chilli flesh into a food processor, then add the feta cheese, olive oil, lemon juice and milk, and blend well. Add a little more milk if the mixture is too stiff, and season with black pepper. Spread the dip on slices of toast, sprinkle a little fresh parsley over the top, and serve.

Variation
The dip is also excellent served with a selection of vegetable crudités, such as carrot, cauliflower, green or red (bell) pepper and celery.

Raw Vegetable Platter

This colourful array of vegetables makes an enticing appetizer when served with a creamy dip – choose a dip with bags of flavour for the best effect.

Serves 6–8

225g/8oz fresh baby corn cobs
175–225g/6–8oz thin asparagus, trimmed
2 red and 2 yellow (bell) peppers, seeded and sliced lengthwise
1 chicory (Belgian endive) head, trimmed and leaves separated
1 small bunch radishes with small leaves
175g/6oz cherry tomatoes
12 quail's eggs, boiled for 3 minutes, drained, refreshed and peeled
aïoli or tapenade, to serve

1 Bring a large pan of water to the boil, add the baby corn cobs and trimmed asparagus and bring back to the boil. Blanch for 1–2 minutes, then drain and cool quickly under cold running water or dip in a bowl of iced water. Drain well.

2 Arrange the corn cobs, asparagus, chicory leaves, radishes and tomatoes on a serving plate together with the quail's eggs.

3 Cover with a damp dish towel until ready to serve. Serve with aïoli or tapenade for dipping.

Cook's Tips

• To make tapenade, place 175g/6oz/1½ cups pitted black olives, 50g/2oz drained anchovy fillets and 30ml/2 tbsp capers in a food processor with 120ml/4fl oz/½ cup olive oil and the finely grated rind of 1 lemon. Lightly process to blend, then season with ground black pepper and a little more oil if it is very dry.

• To make a herby aïoli, beat together 2 egg yolks, 5ml/1 tsp Dijon mustard and 10ml/2 tsp white wine vinegar. Gradually blend in 250ml/8fl oz/1 cup olive oil, a trickle at a time, whisking well after each addition, until thick and smooth. Season with salt and pepper to taste, then stir in 45ml/3 tbsp chopped mixed fresh herbs and 4–5 crushed garlic cloves.

Tomato & Cucumber Salad

Refreshing cucumber slices are coated with a delicious minty cream, then combined with colourful tomatoes to make a tangy salad starter with a difference.

Serves 4–6

1 medium cucumber, peeled and thinly sliced
30ml/2 tbsp white wine vinegar
5–6 ice cubes
90ml/6 tbsp crème fraîche or soured cream
30ml/2 tbsp chopped fresh mint
4 or 5 ripe tomatoes, sliced
salt and ground black pepper
fresh mint sprig, to garnish

1 Place the cucumber in a bowl, sprinkle with a little salt and 15 ml/1 tbsp of the vinegar and toss with the ice cubes. Chill for 1 hour to crisp, then rinse, drain and pat dry.

2 Return the cucumber to the bowl, add the cream, pepper and mint and stir to mix well.

3 Arrange the tomato slices on a serving plate, sprinkle with the remaining vinegar and spoon the cucumber slices into the centre. Serve garnished with a mint sprig.

Cook's Tip

This is delicious served as part of a tapas medley. Try serving with tapas dishes such as salted almonds and marinated olives.

• For salted almonds, mix 1.5ml/¼ tsp cayenne pepper and 30ml/2 tbsp sea salt in a bowl. Melt 25g/1oz/2 tbsp butter with 60ml/4 tbsp olive oil in a frying pan. Add 200g/7oz/1¾ cups blanched almonds and fry for 5 minutes until golden. Toss in the salt mixture to coat, then leave to cool before serving.

• For marinated olives, crush 2.5ml/½ tsp each coriander and fennel seeds in a mortar with a pestle. Work in 2 garlic cloves, then add 5ml/1 tsp each chopped fresh rosemary and parsley, with 15ml/1 tbsp sherry vinegar and 30ml/2 tbsp olive oil. Put 115g/4oz/⅔ cup each black and green olives in a small bowl and pour over the marinade. Cover and chill for up to 1 week.

Raw vegetable platter: Energy 67kcal/281kJ; Protein 4.8g; Carbohydrate 6.6g, of which sugars 5.7g; Fat 2.8g, of which saturates 0.8g; Cholesterol 71mg; Calcium 33mg; Fibre 2.3g; Sodium 353mg
Tomato & cucumber salad: Energy 73kcal/300kJ; Protein 1.1g; Carbohydrate 3.1g, of which sugars 2.9g; Fat 6.3g, of which saturates 4.1g; Cholesterol 17mg; Calcium 25mg; Fibre 0.9g; Sodium 11mg

Olives with Moroccan Marinades

Preserved and fresh lemons provide their own distinct qualities to these appetizers. Start preparations a week in advance to allow the flavours to develop.

Serves 6–8

450g/1lb/2⅔ cups whole olives

For the piquant marinade

45ml/3 tbsp chopped fresh coriander (cilantro)
45ml/3 tbsp chopped fresh parsley
1 garlic clove, finely chopped
good pinch of cayenne pepper
good pinch of ground cumin
30–45ml/2–3 tbsp olive oil
30–45ml/2–3 tbsp lemon juice

For the spicy marinade

60ml/4 tbsp chopped fresh coriander (cilantro)
60ml/4 tbsp chopped fresh parsley
1 garlic clove, finely chopped
5ml/1 tsp grated fresh root ginger
1 red chilli, seeded and sliced
¼ preserved lemon, cut into strips

1 Using the flat side of a large knife blade, crack the olives, hard enough to break the flesh, but taking care not to crack the pits.

2 Place the olives in a bowl of cold water, cover and leave overnight in a cool place to remove the excess brine. The next day, drain them thoroughly and divide among two sterilized screw-top jars.

3 To make the piquant marinade, mix the coriander, parsley and garlic together in a bowl. Add the cayenne pepper and cumin and 30ml/2 tbsp of the olive oil and lemon juice. Add the olives from one jar, mix well and return the marinated olives to the jar. Add more olive oil and lemon juice to cover if necessary. Seal.

4 To make the spicy marinade, mix together the coriander, parsley, garlic, ginger, chilli and preserved lemon. Add the olives from the second jar, mix well and return to the jar. Seal.

5 Store the olives in the refrigerator for at least 1 week before using, shaking the jars occasionally.

Avocado Salad

In India, avocados are called butter fruit, reflecting their subtle taste. This delicate dish makes a good appetizer.

Serves 4

2 avocados
75ml/5 tbsp/⅓ cup natural (plain) yogurt, beaten
115g/4oz cottage cheese with chives
1 garlic clove, crushed
2 green chillies, finely chopped
a little lemon juice
a few lettuce leaves, shredded (a mixture will make a good display)
salt and ground black pepper
paprika and fresh mint leaves, to garnish

1 Cut the avocados in half lengthwise and remove the stones (pits). Gently scoop out the flesh, reserving the skins. Cut the flesh into small cubes.

2 In a bowl, mix the yogurt, cottage cheese, garlic, chillies and salt and pepper and fold in the avocado cubes. Chill.

3 Rub the avocado skins with some lemon juice to prevent discolouration and line each cavity with some shredded lettuce. Top with the chilled avocado mixture, garnish with the paprika and mint leaves and serve immediately.

Variation

Try combining avocado with tropical fruit to make an unusual starter. Halve, stone (pit) and peel 2 avocados, then cut into thick slices. Peel a papaya, cut in half and scoop out the seeds. Set aside 5ml/1tsp seeds and cut the papaya flesh into thick slices. Peel 1 large sweet orange and cut into segments, removing the membranes. Make a dressing by mixing 50ml/2fl oz/¼ cup olive oil with 30ml/2 tbsp fresh lime juice and salt and pepper. Stir in the reserved papaya seeds. Arrange alternate slices of fruit and avocado on individual plates. Top with a little rocket and scatter over thinly sliced red onion rings. Spoon on the dressing and serve immediately.

Olives with Moroccan mariandes: Energy 78kcal/320kJ; Protein 1.1g; Carbohydrate 0.7g, of which sugars 0.4g; Fat 7.9g, of which saturates 1.2g; Cholesterol 0mg; Calcium 55mg; Fibre 2g; Sodium 1017mg
Avocado salad: Energy 160kcal/662kJ; Protein 6.2g; Carbohydrate 3.5g, of which sugars 2.6g; Fat 13.4g, of which saturates 3.4g; Cholesterol 4mg; Calcium 81mg; Fibre 2.2g; Sodium 124mg

Guacamole Salsa in Red Leaves

This lovely, light, summery starter looks especially attractive when it is arranged in individual cups of radicchio leaves.

Serves 4

2 tomatoes
15ml/1 tbsp grated onion
1 garlic clove, crushed
1 green chilli, halved, seeded and chopped
2 ripe avocados
30 ml/2 tbsp olive oil
2.5ml/½ tsp ground cumin
30ml/2 tbsp chopped fresh coriander (cilantro) or parsley
juice of 1 lime
radicchio leaves
salt and ground black pepper
fresh coriander (cilantro) sprigs, to garnish
crusty garlic bread and lime wedges, to serve

1 Using a sharp knife, slash a small cross on the top of the tomatoes, then plunge into a bowl of boiling water for 30 seconds. Refresh in cold water and peel away the skins. Remove the core of each tomato and chop the flesh.

2 Put the tomato flesh into a bowl together with the grated onion, crushed garlic and chopped chilli. Halve the avocados, remove the stones (pits), then scoop the flesh into the bowl, mashing it with a fork.

3 Add the oil, cumin, coriander or parsley and lime juice. Mix well together and season with salt and pepper to taste.

4 Lay the radicchio leaves on a platter and spoon in the salsa. Serve garnished with coriander sprigs and accompanied by garlic bread and lime wedges.

Cook's Tip
Garlic bread is ideal with this salsa. Cut a French loaf into 2.5cm/1in slices, without cutting right through the base. Cream about 115g/4oz butter until soft, then beat in 2–3 crushed garlic cloves. Spread the butter between the slices. Wrap in foil and bake at 180°C/350°F/Gas 4 for about 15 minutes.

Egg-stuffed Tomatoes

This simple dish looks elegant and is incredibly easy to assemble. The herb-flavoured mayonnaise is the perfect foil to the egg and tomato. Served with lots of warmed baguette, it makes a lovely appetizer or quick, light lunch dish.

Serves 4

175ml/6fl oz/¾ cup mayonnaise
30ml/2 tbsp chopped fresh chives
30ml/2 tbsp chopped fresh basil
30ml/2 tbsp chopped fresh parsley
4 hard-boiled eggs
4 ripe tomatoes
salt and ground black pepper
salad leaves, to serve

1 Mix together the mayonnaise and chopped fresh herbs in a small bowl. Transfer the mixture to a small serving dish and set aside.

2 Using an egg slicer or sharp knife, cut the eggs into thin slices, taking care to keep the slices intact.

3 Make deep cuts to within 1cm/½in of the base of each tomato. (There should be the same number of cuts in each tomato as there are slices of each egg.)

4 Fan open the tomatoes and sprinkle them with salt, then carefully insert an egg slice into each slit. Place each stuffed tomato on a plate with a few salad leaves and season with salt and ground black pepper.

5 Serve te tomatoes accompanied by the herb mayonnaise.

Cook's Tip
Tomatoes left to ripen on the vine will have the best flavour so try to buy 'vine-ripened' varieties. Luckily, these are now widely available in supermarkets and more flavourful varieties are becoming easier to find. However, nothing can beat the taste of home-grown, organic tomatoes. You can use any type of tomato for this dish – halved cherry tomatoes will look attractive or use Italian plum tomatoes for an authentic touch.

Guacamole salsa: Energy 189kcal/783kJ; Protein 2.4g; Carbohydrate 4.2g, of which sugars 3.2g; Fat 18.1g, of which saturates 3.5g; Cholesterol 0mg; Calcium 50mg; Fibre 3.8g; Sodium 14mg
Egg-stuffed tomatoes: Energy 309kcal/1276kJ; Protein 7.6g; Carbohydrate 3.6g, of which sugars 3.4g; Fat 29.6g, of which saturates 5.2g; Cholesterol 214mg; Calcium 62mg; Fibre 1.5g; Sodium 223mg

Mango, Tomato & Red Onion Salad

The firm texture of under-ripe mango blends well with the tomato and gives this appetizer a tropical touch.

Serves 4

1 firm under-ripe mango
2 large tomatoes or 1 beef tomato, sliced
½ red onion, sliced into rings
½ cucumber, peeled and thinly sliced

For the dressing

30ml/2 tbsp sunflower or vegetable oil
15ml/1 tbsp lemon juice
1 garlic clove, crushed
2.5ml/½ tsp hot pepper sauce
salt and ground black pepper
snipped chives, to garnish

1 Have the mango lengthwise, cutting either side of the large flat stone (pit). Cut the flesh into slices and then peel the skin away.

2 Arrange the slices of mango, tomato, onion and cucumber on a large serving plate.

3 To make the dressing, blend the oil, lemon juice, garlic, hot pepper sauce and salt and ground black pepper in a blender or food processor. Alternatively, place the ingredients in a small screw-top jar and shake vigorously until all the ingredients are thoroughly combined.

4 Pour the dressing over the prepared salad and serve garnished with snipped chives.

Cook's Tip

A simple way to slice a mango is to take two thick slices from either side of the large flat stone (pit) without peeling the fruit. Slice the flesh of the fruit on each side and then turn them inside out. The slices of flesh will stand proud of the skin and can easily be cut off.

Sun-Dried Tomato & Pepper Salad

This appetizer is very new-wave – a modern Mediterranean dish that bridges the gap between Middle-Eastern and contemporary European styles. It is good served with slices of very fresh bread or wedges of flat bread.

Serves 4–6

10–15 sun-dried tomatoes
60–75ml/4–5 tbsp olive oil
3 yellow (bell) peppers, cut into bitesize pieces
6 garlic cloves, chopped
400g/14oz can chopped tomatoes
5ml/1 tsp fresh thyme leaves, or more to taste
large pinch of sugar
15ml/1 tbsp balsamic vinegar
2–3 capers, rinsed and drained
15ml/1 tbsp chopped fresh parsley, or more to taste
salt and ground black pepper
fresh thyme, to garnish

1 Put the sun-dried tomatoes in a bowl and pour over boiling water to cover. Leave to stand for at least 30 minutes until plumped up and juicy, then drain and cut the tomatoes into halves or quarters.

2 Heat the olive oil in a pan, add the peppers and cook for 5–7 minutes until lightly browned but not too soft.

3 Add half the chopped garlic, the tomatoes, thyme and sugar and cook over a high heat, stirring occasionally, until the mixture is reduced to a thick paste. Season with salt and ground black pepper to taste. Stir in the sun-dried tomatoes, balsamic vinegar, capers and the remaining chopped garlic. Leave to cool to room temperature.

4 Serve the salad at room temperature, heaped into a serving bowl and sprinkled with parsley. Garnish with fresh thyme.

Cook's Tip

Do not waste the tomato-flavoured soaking liquid – it can be used to add flavour to soups or sauces.

Mango, tomato & red onion salad:: Energy 89kcal/369kJ; Protein 1.1g; Carbohydrate 8.6g, of which sugars 7.9g; Fat 5.8g, of which saturates 0.8g; Cholesterol 0mg; Calcium 17mg; Fibre 1.9g; Sodium 7mg
Sun-dried tomato & pepper salad: Energy 125kcal/520kJ; Protein 2.7g; Carbohydrate 11g, of which sugars 9.6g; Fat 8.1g, of which saturates 1.2g; Cholesterol 0mg; Calcium 34mg; Fibre 3.2g; Sodium 33mg

Roasted Tomatoes & Mozzarella with Basil Oil

The basil oil needs to be made just before serving to retain its fresh colour.

Serves 4

olive oil, for brushing
6 large plum tomatoes
350g/12oz fresh mozzarella cheese, cut into 8–12 slices
fresh basil leaves, to garnish

For the basil oil

25 fresh basil leaves
60ml/4 tbsp extra virgin olive oil
1 garlic clove, crushed

For the salad

90g/3½ oz/4 cups salad leaves
50g/2oz/2 cups mixed salad herbs, such as coriander (cilantro), basil and rocket (arugula)
25g/1oz/3 tbsp pumpkin seeds
25g/1oz/3 tbsp sunflower seeds
60ml/4 tbsp extra virgin olive oil
15ml/1 tbsp balsamic vinegar
2.5ml/½ tsp Dijon mustard

1 Preheat the oven to 200°C/400°F/Gas 6 and oil a baking sheet. Cut the tomatoes in half lengthwise and remove the seeds. Place skin-side down on a baking sheet and roast for 20 minutes or until the tomatoes are tender.

2 Meanwhile, make the basil oil. Place the basil leaves, olive oil and garlic in a food processor and process until smooth. Transfer to a bowl and chill.

3 Put the salad leaves and herbs in a large bowl and toss lightly to mix. Toast the pumpkin and sunflower seeds in a dry frying pan over a medium heat for 2 minutes until golden, tossing frequently. Allow to cool before sprinkling over the salad.

4 Whisk together the oil, vinegar and mustard, then pour the dressing over the salad and toss until the leaves are well coated.

5 For each serving, place the tomato halves on top of two or three slices of mozzarella and drizzle over the basil oil. Season well. Garnish with basil leaves and serve with the salad.

Spiced Aubergine, Tomato & Cucumber Salad

Packed with Middle-Eastern ingredients, this lovely salad would be perfect to serve before a main course of chargrilled tofu. Simply serve with warm pitta bread and your guests will be more than satisfied.

Serves 4

2 small aubergines (eggplants), sliced
75ml/5 tbsp olive oil
60ml/4 tbsp red wine vinegar
2 garlic cloves, crushed
15ml/1 tbsp lemon juice
2.5ml/½ tsp ground cumin
2.5ml/½ tsp ground coriander
7 well-flavoured tomatoes
½ cucumber
30ml/2 tbsp natural (plain) yogurt
salt and ground black pepper
chopped flat leaf parsley, to garnish

1 Preheat the grill (broiler). Brush all the aubergine slices lightly with some of the oil and cook under a high heat, turning once, until golden and tender. Cut each slice into quarters.

2 In a bowl, mix together the remaining oil, vinegar, garlic, lemon juice, cumin and coriander. Season and mix thoroughly. Add the warm aubergines, stir well and chill for at least 2 hours.

3 Slice or quarter the tomatoes and slice the cucumber finely. Add both cucumber and tomato to the aubergine mixture.

4 Transfer the aubergine mixture to a serving dish and spoon the natural yogurt over the top. Sprinkle with chopped flat leaf parsley and serve immediately.

Variation

An equally delicious warm salad can be made by dicing the aubergines (eggplants) and frying them in olive oil with 1 chopped onion and 2 crushed garlic cloves. Then stir in 5–10ml/1–2 tsp mild curry powder and 3 chopped tomatoes. Cook until soft, then serve with natural (plain) yogurt.

Roasted tomatoes & mozzarella: Energy 525kcal/2174kJ; Protein 20.2g; Carbohydrate 7g, of which sugars 4.8g; Fat 46.4g, of which saturates 15.9g; Cholesterol 51mg; Calcium 371mg; Fibre 2.8g; Sodium 381mg
Spiced aubergine & tomato salad: Energy 174kcal/722kJ; Protein 2.6g; Carbohydrate 8.1g, of which sugars 7.6g; Fat 14.8g, of which saturates 2.3g; Cholesterol 0mg; Calcium 47mg; Fibre 4g; Sodium 28mg

Leek & Grilled Pepper Salad with Goat's Cheese

This is a perfect dish for entertaining, as the salad actually benefits from being made in advance.

Serves 6

675g/1½ lb young leeks
15ml/1 tbsp olive oil
2 large red (bell) peppers, halved and seeded
few fresh thyme sprigs, chopped
4 x 1cm/½in slices goat's cheese
75g/3oz/1½ cups fine dry white breadcrumbs
vegetable oil, for shallow frying
45ml/3 tbsp chopped fresh flat leaf parsley
salt and ground black pepper

For the dressing

75ml/5 tbsp extra virgin olive oil
1 small garlic clove, finely chopped
5ml/1 tsp Dijon mustard
15ml/1 tbsp red wine vinegar

1 Preheat the grill (broiler). Bring a pan of lightly salted water to the boil and cook the leeks for 3–4 minutes. Drain, cut into 10cm/4in lengths and place in a bowl. Add the olive oil, toss to coat, then season to taste.

2 Place the leeks on a grill rack and grill (broil) for 3–4 minutes on each side. Set the leeks aside.

3 Place the peppers on the grill rack, skin side up, and grill until blackened and blistered. Place them in a bowl, cover with crumpled kitchen paper and leave for 10 minutes. Rub off the skin and cut the flesh into strips. Place in a bowl and add the leeks, thyme and a little pepper.

4 To make the dressing, shake all the ingredients together in a screw-top jar, adding salt and pepper to taste. Pour the dressing over the leek mixture, cover and chill for several hours.

5 Roll the cheese slices in the breadcrumbs, pressing them in so that the cheese is well coated. Chill the cheese for 1 hour. Heat a little oil and fry the cheese until golden on both sides. Drain and cool, then cut into bitesize pieces. Toss the cheese and parsley into the salad and serve at room temperature.

Grilled Leek & Courgette Salad with Feta & Mint

Bursting with tangy flavours, this makes a delicious summery appetizer. Try to find genuine ewe's milk feta for the best flavour.

Serves 6

12 slender, baby leeks
6 small courgettes (zucchini)
90ml/6 tbsp extra virgin olive oil
finely shredded rind and juice of ½ lemon
1–2 garlic cloves, finely chopped
½ fresh red chilli, seeded and diced
pinch of caster (superfine) sugar (optional)
50g/2oz/½ cup black olives, pitted and roughly chopped
30ml/2 tbsp chopped fresh mint
150g/5oz feta cheese, sliced or crumbled
salt and ground black pepper
fresh mint leaves, to garnish

1 Bring a large pan of salted water to the boil. Add the leeks and cook for 2–3 minutes. Drain, refresh under cold water, then squeeze out excess water and leave to drain.

2 Cut the courgettes in half lengthwise. Place in a colander, adding 5ml/1 tsp salt to the layers, and leave to drain for 45 minutes. Rinse and dry thoroughly on kitchen paper.

3 Preheat the grill (broiler). Toss the leeks and courgettes in 30ml/2 tbsp of the oil. Grill (broil) the leeks for 2–3 minutes on each side and the courgettes for about 5 minutes on each side. Cut the leeks into serving pieces and place them in a shallow dish with the courgettes.

4 Place the remaining oil in a small bowl and whisk in the lemon rind, 15ml/1 tbsp of the lemon juice, the garlic, chilli and a pinch of sugar, if using. Season to taste with salt and pepper. Add more lemon juice to taste.

5 Pour the dressing over the leeks and courgettes. Stir in the olives and mint, then set aside to marinate for a few hours, turning once or twice. Just before serving, spoon the salad on to individual serving plates, add the feta and garnish with mint.

Leek & grilled pepper salad: Energy 265kcal/1100kJ; Protein 5.7g; Carbohydrate 17g, of which sugars 6.5g; Fat 19.7g, of which saturates 3.9g; Cholesterol 8mg; Calcium 60mg; Fibre 3.7g; Sodium 174mg
Leek & courgette salad: Energy 197kcal/812kJ; Protein 6.2g; Carbohydrate 3.4g, of which sugars 2.9g; Fat 17.6g, of which saturates 5.3g; Cholesterol 18mg; Calcium 140mg; Fibre 2.6g; Sodium 552mg

Salad of Puréed Aubergines

In the heat of high summer, this Middle-Eastern dish makes a surprisingly refreshing appetizer. To be strictly authentic, the aubergines should be grilled over charcoal.

Serves 4

3 large aubergines (eggplants), about 900g/2lb total weight
15ml/1 tbsp roughly chopped onion
2 garlic cloves, crushed
juice of ½ lemon, or a little more
90–105ml/6–7 tbsp extra virgin olive oil
1 ripe tomato, peeled, seeded and finely diced
salt and ground black pepper
finely chopped fresh flat leaf parsley, to garnish
chicory (Belgian endive) leaves and black and green olives, to serve

1 Preheat the oven to 180°C/350°F/Gas 4. Prick the aubergines with a fork and lay them directly on the oven shelves. Roast for 1 hour, or until soft, turning them over twice during cooking.

2 When the aubergines are cool enough to handle, cut them in half. Spoon the flesh into a food processor and add the onion, garlic and lemon juice. Season with salt and ground black pepper and process until smooth.

3 With the motor running, drizzle in the olive oil through the feeder tube, until the mixture forms a smooth paste. Taste the mixture and adjust the seasoning.

4 Spoon the mixture into a bowl and stir in the diced tomato.

5 Cover and chill for 1 hour before serving. Garnish with chopped fresh flat leaf parsley and serve with fresh, washed chicory leaves to scoop up the purée and bowls of olives.

Cook's Tip
You can chargrill the aubergines instead of using the oven. Prick them and grill over a low to medium heat for at least 1 hour.

Grilled Onion & Aubergine Salad with Garlic & Tahini Dressing

This is a deliciously smoky salad that balances sweet and sharp flavours. It makes a substantial appetizer, served with hot pitta bread.

Serves 6

3 aubergines (eggplants), cut into 1cm/½ in thick slices
675g/1½lb onions, thickly sliced
75–90ml/5–6 tbsp olive oil
45ml/3 tbsp roughly chopped flat leaf parsley
45ml/3 tbsp pine nuts, toasted
salt and ground black pepper

For the dressing
2 garlic cloves, crushed
150ml/¼ pint/⅔ cup light tahini paste
juice of 1–2 lemons
45–60ml/3–4 tbsp water

1 Place the aubergines on a rack or in a colander and sprinkle generously with salt. Leave to drain for 45–60 minutes, then rinse under cold running water and pat dry with kitchen paper.

2 Preheat the grill (broiler). Thread the onions on to skewers or place them in an oiled wire grill (broiler) cage.

3 Brush the aubergines and onions with about 45ml/3 tbsp of the oil and grill (broil) for 6–8 minutes on each side. Brush with more oil, if necessary, when you turn them. The vegetables should be browned and soft.

4 Arrange the grilled vegetables on a serving dish and season with salt and black pepper to taste. Sprinkle with the remaining oil if they seem dry.

5 To make the dressing, crush the garlic in a mortar with a pinch of salt and gradually work in the tahini. Gradually work in the juice of 1 lemon, then the water. Taste and add more lemon juice if necessary. Thin with more water to make it fairly runny.

6 Drizzle the dressing over the salad and leave for 30–60 minutes, then sprinkle with the chopped parsley and pine nuts. Serve immediately at room temperature, not chilled.

Puréed aubergines: Energy 190Kcal/788kJ; Protein 2.3g; Carbohydrate 6.7g, of which sugars 5.9g; Fat 17.5g, of which saturates 2.6g; Cholesterol 0mg; Calcium 28mg; Fibre 4.9g; Sodium 7mg
Grilled onion & aubergine salad: Energy 294kcal/1216kJ; Protein 7.2g; Carbohydrate 11.8g, of which sugars 8.6g; Fat 24.6g, of which saturates 3.5g; Cholesterol 0mg; Calcium 224mg; Fibre 6g; Sodium 13mg

Pear & Parmesan Salad with Poppy Seed Dressing

This is a good salad when pears are at their seasonal best. Drizzle them with a poppy-seed dressing and top them with shavings of Parmesan cheese.

Serves 4

4 just-ripe dessert pears
50g/2oz piece of Parmesan cheese
watercress, to garnish
water biscuits (crackers) or rye bread, to serve (optional)

For the dressing

30ml/2 tbsp cider vinegar or white wine vinegar
2.5ml/½ tsp soft light brown sugar
good pinch of dried thyme
30ml/2 tbsp extra virgin olive oil
15ml/1 tbsp sunflower oil
15ml/1 tbsp poppy seeds
salt and ground black pepper

1 Cut the pears into quarters and remove the cores. Peel the pears if you wish, although they look more attractive (and have more fibre) unpeeled.

2 Cut each pear quarter in half lengthwise and arrange them on four small serving plates.

3 To make the dressing, mix the vinegar, sugar and thyme in a bowl. Gradually whisk in the olive oil, then the sunflower oil. Season with salt and pepper, then add the poppy seeds.

4 Trickle the dressing over the pears. Shave Parmesan over the top and garnish with watercress. Serve with water biscuits or thinly sliced rye bread, if you like.

Variation

Blue cheese and pears have a natural affinity. Stilton, Dolcelatte, Gorgonzola or Danish Blue can be used instead of Parmesan. Allow about 200g/7oz and cut into cubes.

Minted Melon & Grapefruit Cocktail

Melon is always a popular appetizer. Here the sweet and delicate flavour is complemented by the clean taste of citrus fruit and a simple dressing.

Serves 4

1 small Galia melon, about 1kg/2¼lb
2 pink grapefruits
1 yellow grapefruit
5ml/1 tsp Dijon mustard
5ml/1 tsp raspberry or sherry vinegar
5ml/1 tsp clear honey
15ml/1 tbsp chopped fresh mint
fresh mint sprigs, to garnish

1 Cut the melon in half and, using a teaspoon, scoop out and discard the seeds. Use a melon baller to scoop out the flesh.

2 Using a sharp knife, peel all three grapefruits and cut away all the white pith. Remove the segments by cutting between the membranes, holding the fruit over a bowl as you cut it to catch any juice.

3 Whisk the mustard, vinegar, honey, chopped mint and grapefruit juice together in a mixing bowl. Add the melon balls and grapefruit segments and mix well. Chill for 30 minutes.

4 Ladle the salad into four individual dishes, garnish each one with a sprig of fresh mint and serve immediately.

Cook's Tips

- *When buying a Galia melon look for an orange tint that turns more yellow when ripe. Apply pressure with your thumbs on either side of the melon and it should give a little. Choose melons that are heavy and have no bruises.*
- *Mix the salad carefully, the melon balls and grapefruit segments are delicate and will break up easily, making the salad look unattractive.*

Pear & Parmesan salad: Energy 240kcal/996kJ; Protein 6.1g; Carbohydrate 16.4g, of which sugars 15.7g; Fat 17g, of which saturates 4.2g; Cholesterol 13mg; Calcium 171mg; Fibre 3.5g; Sodium 141mg
Minted melon & grapefruit cocktail: Energy 101kcal/429kJ; Protein 2.3g; Carbohydrate 23.2g, of which sugars 23.2g; Fat 0.5g, of which saturates 0g; Cholesterol 0mg; Calcium 61mg; Fibre 2.6g; Sodium 118mg

Rocket & Grilled Goat's Cheese Salad

Simple and delicious – peppery leaves topped with grilled cheese croûtons.

Serves 4

4 slices French bread
15ml/1 tbsp extra virgin olive oil
15ml/1 tbsp sunflower oil
225g/8oz cylinder-shaped goat's cheese
generous handfuls of rocket (arugula) leaves
115g/4oz frisée leaves
salt and ground black pepper

For the sauce

45ml/3 tbsp apricot jam
60ml/4 tbsp white wine
5ml/1 tsp Dijon mustard

For the dressing

45ml/3 tbsp walnut oil
15ml/1 tbsp lemon juice

1 Fry the slices of French bread in olive oil, on one side only, until lightly golden. Transfer to a plate lined with kitchen paper and set aside.

2 To make the sauce, heat the jam in a small pan until warm but not boiling. Sieve into a clean pan, to remove the pieces of fruit, then stir in the white wine and mustard. Heat gently and keep warm until ready to serve.

3 Blend the walnut oil and lemon juice and season with a little salt and pepper.

4 Preheat the grill (broiler) a few minutes before serving. Cut the goat's cheese into 50g/2oz rounds and place each piece on a slice of bread, toasted side down. Grill until the cheese melts.

5 Toss the rocket and curly endive leaves in walnut dressing and arrange on individual plates. Top with cheese croûtons and pour over a little of the apricot dressing, then serve.

Cook's Tip
Look for small goat's cheese logs that can be cut into halves.

Pears with Cashel Blue Cream

The Irish cheese Cashel Blue is the perfect partner to ripe, juicy pears – and it is now widely available from specialist cheese suppliers.

Serves 6

115g/4oz fresh cream cheese
75g/3oz Cashel Blue cheese
30–45ml/2–3 tbsp single (light) cream
115g/4oz/1 cup roughly chopped walnuts
6 ripe pears
15ml/1 tbsp lemon juice
mixed salad leaves, such as frisée, oakleaf lettuce and radicchio
6 cherry tomatoes
sea salt and ground black pepper
walnut halves and sprigs of fresh flat leaf parsley, to garnish

For the dressing

juice of 1 lemon
a little finely grated lemon rind
pinch of caster (superfine) sugar
60ml/4 tbsp olive oil

1 Mash the cream cheese and Cashel Blue cheese together in a mixing bowl with a good grinding of black pepper, then blend in the cream to make a smooth mixture. Add 25g/1oz/¼ cup chopped walnuts and mix to distribute evenly. Cover and chill.

2 Peel and halve the pears and scoop out the core. Put them into a bowl of water with the lemon juice to prevent them from browning.

3 To make the dressing, whisk the lemon juice, lemon rind, caster sugar and olive oil together in a bowl and season with salt and pepper to taste.

4 Arrange a bed of salad leaves on six plates – shallow soup plates are ideal – add a tomato to each and sprinkle over the remaining chopped walnuts.

5 Drain the pears well and pat dry with kitchen paper, then turn them in the prepared dressing and arrange, hollow side up, on the salad leaves. Divide the Cashel Blue mixture between the six halved pears and spoon the rest of the dressing over the top. Garnish each pear with a walnut half and a sprig of parsley.

Rocket & grilled goat's cheese salad: Energy 453kcal/1890kJ; Protein 15.9g; Carbohydrate 31.7g, of which sugars 10.4g; Fat 29.3g, of which saturates 11.7g; Cholesterol 52mg; Calcium 139mg; Fibre 1.4g; Sodium 592mg
Pears with Cashel Blue: Energy 331Kcal/1373kJ; Protein 6.7g; Carbohydrate 16.3g, of which sugars 16.1g; Fat 27g, of which saturates 9.8g; Cholesterol 30mg; Calcium 120mg; Fibre 4.1g; Sodium 219mg

Mozzarella, Tomato & Basil Salad

This very popular first course salad is considered rather patriotic in Italy, as its three ingredients are the colours of the national flag. It is especially divine with a glass of chilled Pinot Grigio and warmed ciabatta bread.

Serves 4
4 large tomatoes
225g/8oz/2 cups mozzarella cheese, made from either cow or buffalo milk
8–10 fresh basil leaves
60ml/4 tbsp extra virgin olive oil
salt and ground black pepper

1 Using a sharp knife, slice the tomatoes into thick even rounds.

2 Slice the mozzarella into thick, even rounds the same size as the tomato slices.

3 Arrange the tomatoes and cheese in overlapping slices on a serving dish. Decorate with basil leaves.

4 Sprinkle the salad with extra virgin olive oil and a little salt.

5 Serve the salad at room temperature once it has had a few minutes to take on the flavour of the olive oil. Pass the black pepper around separately.

Cook's Tips

- *In Italy, the most sought-after mozzarella is made from the milk of water buffalo as it has a far superior texture to other kinds of mozzarella.*
- *Mozzarella is sold in brine, whey or water solution. Keep it in the liquid until ready to use and then consume within 2–3 days.*
- *Mozzarella is best served at room temperature. Remove it from the refrigerator 2–3 hours before using.*
- *When slicing tomatoes, a good serrated knife is better than a flat-edge knife. If you use a flat-edge knife, make sure it is very sharp to prevent squashing or bruising the fruit.*

Jicama, Chilli & Lime Salad

A very tasty, crisp vegetable, the jicama is sometimes called the Mexican potato. Unlike potato, however, it can be eaten raw and here it is transformed into a zingy salad appetizer to serve with drinks.

Serves 4
1 jicama
2.5ml/½ tsp salt
2 fresh Serrano chillies
2 limes

1 Peel the jicama with a potato peeler or knife, then cut it into 2cm/¾in cubes. Put the cubes in a large bowl, add the salt and toss well to coat.

2 Cut the chillies in half, scrape out the seeds with a sharp knife, then cut the flesh into fine strips. Grate one of the limes thinly, removing only the coloured part of the skin, then cut the lime in half and squeeze the juice.

3 Add the chillies, lime rind and juice to the jicama and mix thoroughly to ensure that all the jicama cubes are coated. Cut the other lime into wedges.

4 Cover the salad and chill for at least 1 hour before serving with lime wedges. If the salad is to be served as an appetizer with drinks, transfer the jicama cubes to little bowls and offer them with cocktail sticks (toothpicks) for spearing.

Cook's Tips

- *Look for jicama in Oriental supermarkets, as it is widely used in Chinese cooking. It goes by several names and you may find it labelled as either yam bean or Chinese turnip.*
- *Take care when handling fresh chillies as the juice can burn sensitive skin. Wear rubber gloves to protect your hands or wash your hands very thoroughly after preparation. Be careful also not to touch your eyes when preparing chillies as the juices can cause unpleasant stinging.*

Mozzarella, tomato & basil salad: Energy 261kcal/1080kJ; Protein 11.2g; Carbohydrate 3.1g, of which sugars 3.1g; Fat 22.7g, of which saturates 9.4g; Cholesterol 33mg; Calcium 211mg; Fibre 1g; Sodium 231mg
Jicama, chilli & lime salad: Energy 6kcal/26kJ; Protein 0.4g; Carbohydrate 0.8g, of which sugars 0.8g; Fat 0.2g, of which saturates 0g; Cholesterol 0mg; Calcium 32mg; Fibre 0.8g; Sodium 45mg

Stuffed Vine Leaves with Rice

Start a meal on a sunny note with these traditional Greek delicacies.

Serves 4–6
50 fresh or 225g/8oz preserved vine leaves
175g/6oz/scant 1 cup long grain rice
350g/12oz onions, very finely diced
4–5 spring onions (scallions), green and white parts, thinly sliced
30ml/2 tbsp pine nuts, toasted
60ml/4 tbsp finely chopped fresh dill
45ml/3 tbsp finely chopped fresh mint
30ml/2 tbsp finely chopped fresh flat leaf parsley
150ml/¼ pint/⅔ cup extra virgin olive oil
juice of 1 lemon
450ml/¾ pint/scant 2 cups hot water
salt and ground black pepper
4–6 lemon wedges, to serve

1 If using fresh leaves, blanch them briefly in batches in a pan of boiling water, then lift out with a slotted spoon after a few seconds and drain in a colander. They should just be wilted to make them pliable; not cooked. Preserved leaves can be extremely salty and must be rinsed well before being immersed in a bowl of hot water. Leave the vine leaves in the water for 4–5 minutes, then drain, rinse and drain again.

2 Put the rice in a large bowl. Add the onions, spring onions, pine nuts, dill, mint and parsley. Mix well, then stir in half the olive oil and half the lemon juice. Season with salt and pepper.

3 Line the bottom of a wide pan with 2–3 of the vine leaves. Spread another vine leaf out on a board, veined side up, and place 15ml/1 tsp of the stuffing near the stalk end. Fold the two opposite sides of the leaf over the stuffing and then roll up tightly from the stalk end. Make more rolls in the same way and pack them tightly together in circles in the pan.

4 Mix the remaining oil and lemon juice and pour over the rolls. Invert a small plate on top to hold in place. Carefully pour in the hot water, cover tightly and simmer gently for 1 hour. Serve hot or at room temperature with lemon wedges.

Zahlouk with Pale Courgette & Cauliflower Salad

Serve Zahlouk, a delicious, spicy aubergine and tomato appetizer, with plenty of flat bread for scooping it up.

Serves 4
For the zahlouk
3 large aubergines (eggplants), peeled and cubed
3–4 large tomatoes, peeled and chopped to a pulp
5ml/1 tsp sugar
3–4 garlic cloves, crushed
60ml/4 tbsp olive oil
juice of 1 lemon
scant 5ml/1 tsp harissa
5ml/1 tsp cumin seeds, roasted and ground
small bunch flat leaf parsley, chopped
salt and ground black pepper

For the courgette and cauliflower salad
60ml/4 tbsp olive oil
2–3 small courgettes (zucchini), thickly sliced
1 cauliflower, broken into florets
juice of 1 lemon
2–3 garlic cloves, crushed
small bunch parsley, finely chopped

1 To make the zahlouk, boil the aubergines in salted water for about 15 minutes, until they are very soft. Drain and squeeze out the excess water, then chop and mash them with a fork.

2 Put the pulped tomatoes in a pan, stir in the sugar and cook over a gentle heat until they are reduced to a thick sauce. Add the mashed aubergines. Stir in the garlic, olive oil, lemon juice, harissa, cumin and parsley until well mixed. Season to taste.

3 To make the courgette and cauliflower salad, heat about half the olive oil in a heavy pan and brown the courgettes on both sides. Drain on kitchen paper.

4 Meanwhile, steam the cauliflower over boiling water for 7–10 minutes until tender. While the cauliflower is still warm, mash it lightly in a bowl and mix in the remaining olive oil, half the lemon juice and the garlic. Add the courgettes and parsley with the remaining lemon juice and season to taste. Serve the salad at room temperature, with the zahlouk.

Stuffed vine leaves: Energy 339kcal/1407kJ; Protein 5.8g; Carbohydrate 32.2g, of which sugars 7.3g; Fat 20.9g, of which saturates 2.7g; Cholesterol 0mg; Calcium 95mg; Fibre 3.4g; Sodium 14mg
Zahlouk: Energy 296kcal/1225kJ; Protein 7.5g; Carbohydrate 12.7g, of which sugars 10.4g; Fat 24.3g, of which saturates 3.7g; Cholesterol 0mg; Calcium 90mg; Fibre 6.9g; Sodium 23mg

Creamy Cucumber & Walnut Appetizer

In this Bulgarian salad, diced cucumber is bathed in a luscious garlicky yogurt dressing and topped with chopped walnuts for a delicious contrast in texture and flavour. Serve with chunks of rustic bread as a fresh-tasting alternative to a meat or fish pâté.

Serves 6

1 large cucumber
3–5 garlic cloves, finely chopped
250ml/8fl oz/1 cup soured cream or 120ml/4fl oz/½ cup Greek (US strained plain) yogurt mixed with 120ml/4fl oz/½ cup double (heavy) cream
250ml/8fl oz/1 cup thick Greek (US strained plain) yogurt
2–3 large pinches of dried dill or 30–45ml/2–3 tbsp chopped fresh dill
45–60ml/3–4 tbsp chopped walnuts
salt
sprig of dill, to garnish (optional)

1 Do not peel the cucumber. Using a sharp knife, dice it finely and place in a large mixing bowl.

2 Add the garlic, soured cream or yogurt and cream, yogurt and dill and season with salt. Mix all the ingredients together, then cover and chill.

3 Serve sprinkled with walnuts. Garnish with dill, if you like.

Cook's Tip
When made with very thick Greek yogurt, this appetizer can be shaped into balls and served on salad leaves.

Variation
For a Greek version, to serve as part of a mezze, add chopped fresh mint instead of dill, omit the walnuts and serve with olives and pitta bread.

Mint & Parsley Tahini Salad

The almost dry flavour of tahini marries wonderfully with the fresh herbs and subtle spices in this refreshing appetizer.

Serves 4–6

115g/4oz/½ cup tahini paste
3 garlic cloves, chopped
½ bunch (about 20g/¾oz) fresh mint, chopped
½ bunch (about 20g/¾oz) fresh coriander (cilantro), chopped
½ bunch (about 20g/¾oz) fresh flat leaf parsley, chopped
juice of ½ lemon, or to taste
pinch of ground cumin
pinch of ground turmeric
pinch of ground cardamom seeds
cayenne pepper, to taste
salt

To serve
extra virgin olive oil
warmed pitta bread
black olives
raw vegetable sticks, such as carrots, cucumber, celery and cauliflower

1 Combine the tahini with the chopped garlic, fresh herbs and lemon juice in a bowl. Taste and add a little more lemon juice, if you like. Stir in a little water if the mixture seems too dense and thick. Alternatively, place the ingredients in a food processor. Process briefly, then stir in a little water if required.

2 Stir in the cumin, turmeric and cardamom to taste, then season with salt and cayenne pepper.

3 To serve, spoon into a shallow bowl or onto plates and drizzle with olive oil. Serve with warmed pitta bread, olives and raw vegetables.

Cook's Tip
Tahini is a creamy-textured, oily paste made from ground sesame seeds. Popular in Middle-Eastern cooking, it is used to give a nutty flavour to dishes. It is widely available from wholefood shops and delicatessens, as well as from some supermarkets. Tahini paste is an integral flavouring in the famous chickpea dip, hummus.

Cucumber & walnut appetizer: Energy 167kcal/688kJ; Protein 4.9g; Carbohydrate 5.7g, of which sugars 5.6g; Fat 14g, of which saturates 5.8g; Cholesterol 26mg; Calcium 148mg; Fibre 0.9g; Sodium 56mg
Mint & parsley tahini salad: Energy 121kcal/500kJ; Protein 4g; Carbohydrate 0.5g, of which sugars 0.4g; Fat 11.5g, of which saturates 1.6g; Cholesterol 0mg; Calcium 157mg; Fibre 2.2g; Sodium 8mg

Parsley & Rocket Salad with Black Olive & Garlic Dressing

A light dish, but full of flavour, this salad is perfect for a lunchtime snack. Use the best Parmesan cheese – parmigiano reggiano – for a great taste experience.

Serves 6

1 garlic clove, halved
115g/4oz good white bread, cut into 1cm/½in thick slices
45ml/3 tbsp olive oil, plus extra for shallow frying
75g/3oz rocket (arugula) leaves
75g/3oz baby spinach
25g/1oz flat leaf parsley, stalks removed
45ml/3 tbsp salted capers, rinsed and dried
40g/1½oz Parmesan cheese, pared into shavings

For the dressing

25ml/5 tsp black olive paste
1 garlic clove, finely chopped
5ml/1 tsp Dijon mustard
75ml/5 tbsp olive oil
10ml/2 tsp balsamic vinegar
ground black pepper

1 To make the dressing, whisk the black olive paste, garlic and mustard together in a bowl. Gradually whisk in the olive oil, then the vinegar. Adjust the seasoning with black pepper – the dressing should be sufficiently salty.

2 Heat the oven to 190°C/375°F/Gas 5. Rub the halved garlic clove over the bread and cut or tear the slices into bitesize croûtons. Toss them in the oil and place on a small baking tray. Bake for 10–15 minutes, stirring once, until golden brown. Cool on kitchen paper.

3 Mix the rocket, spinach and parsley in a large salad bowl.

4 Heat a shallow layer of olive oil in a frying pan. Add the capers and fry briefly until crisp. Scoop out straight away and drain on kitchen paper.

5 Toss the dressing and croûtons into the salad and divide it among 6 bowls or plates. Scatter the Parmesan shavings and the fried capers over the top and serve immediately.

Avocado, Red Onion & Spinach Salad

The simple lemon dressing gives a sharp tang to this sophisticated salad, while polenta croûtons, with their crunchy golden exterior and soft centre, add a contrast of both taste and texture.

Serves 4

1 large red onion, cut into wedges
300g/11oz ready-made polenta, cut into 1cm/½in cubes
olive oil, for brushing
225g/8oz baby spinach leaves
1 avocado
5ml/1 tsp lemon juice

For the dressing

60ml/4 tbsp extra virgin olive oil
juice of ½ lemon
salt and ground black pepper

1 Preheat the oven to 200°C/400°F/Gas 6. Place the onion wedges and polenta cubes on a lightly oiled baking sheet and bake for 25 minutes, or until the onion is tender and the polenta is crisp and golden, turning everything frequently to prevent sticking. Leave to cool slightly.

2 Meanwhile, make the dressing. Place the olive oil and lemon juice in a screw-top jar. Add salt and pepper to taste, close the jar tightly and shake vigorously to combine.

3 Place the spinach in a serving bowl. Peel, stone (pit) and slice the avocado, then toss the slices in the lemon juice to prevent them from discolouring. Add to the spinach with the onions.

4 Pour the dressing over the salad and toss gently. Sprinkle the polenta croûtons on top or hand them round separately.

Cook's Tip

Polenta is a type of cornmeal, popular in Italian cooking. To make polenta cubes, simply cook the polenta grains in salted water, according to the packet instructions, until thick. Spread the polenta on a board, leave to cool, then cut into cubes.

Parsley & rocket salad: Energy 262kcal/1084kJ; Protein 9.8g; Carbohydrate 12.7g, of which sugars 3.5g; Fat 19.3g, of which saturates 3.7g; Cholesterol 7mg; Calcium 437mg; Fibre 4.5g; Sodium 565mg
Avocado, red onion & spinach: Energy 442kcal/1838kJ; Protein 9.3g; Carbohydrate 57.4g, of which sugars 1.8g; Fat 18.8g, of which saturates 2.7g; Cholesterol 0mg; Calcium 105mg; Fibre 3.9g; Sodium 81mg

Moroccan Vegetable Salad

This fresh and invigorating salad makes a satisfying vegetarian dish. Arrange it carefully for the best effect.

Serves 4

1 large cucumber, thinly sliced
2 cold, boiled potatoes, sliced
1 each red, yellow and green (bell) peppers, seeded and thinly sliced
300g/11oz/2⅔ cups pitted olives
½–1 hot fresh chilli, chopped or 2–3 shakes of cayenne pepper
3–5 garlic cloves, chopped
3 spring onions (scallions), sliced or 1 red onion, finely chopped
60–90ml/4–6 tbsp extra virgin olive oil
15–30ml/1–2 tbsp white wine vinegar
juice of ½ lemon, or to taste
15–30ml/1–2 tbsp chopped fresh mint leaves
15–30ml/1–2 tbsp chopped fresh coriander (cilantro) leaves
salt (optional)

1 Arrange the cucumber, potato and pepper slices and the pitted olives on a serving plate or in a dish.

2 Sprinkle the chopped fresh chilli or cayenne pepper over the salad and season with salt, if you like. (Olives tend to be very salty so you may not wish to add any extra salt.)

3 Sprinkle the garlic, onions, olive oil, vinegar and lemon juice over the salad. Chill before serving, sprinkled with the chopped mint leaves and coriander leaves.

Cook's Tip
For a satisfying, well-balanced vegetarian meal, serve this salad with a spicy lentil soup and chunks of wholemeal (whole-wheat) bread, or Italian focaccia, flavoured with onions, olives or sun-dried tomato.

Variation
Serve the salad garnished with sliced or diced cooked beetroot (beet) for extra colour and a delicious flavour.

Sun-ripened Tomato & Feta Salad with Lamb's Lettuce

This tasty summer salad is a version of the traditional Greek salad. The addition of plenty of lamb's lettuce, with its dark narrow leaves and distinctive tangy flavour, gives a deliciously zesty twist.

Serves 4

225g/8oz tomatoes
1 green (bell) pepper, seeded and sliced into thin ribbons
1 red onion, thinly sliced
1 piece of cucumber, about 15cm/6in in length, peeled and sliced in rounds
150g/5oz feta cheese, cubed
a large handful of lamb's lettuce (corn salad)
8–10 black olives
90–105ml/6–7 tbsp extra virgin olive oil
15ml/1 tbsp lemon juice
1.5ml/¼ tsp dried oregano
salt and ground black pepper

1 Cut the tomatoes into quarters and place them in a large salad bowl.

2 Add the green pepper, red onion, cucumber, feta, lamb's lettuce and black olives.

3 Sprinkle the extra-virgin olive oil, lemon juice and oregano on top. Add salt and ground black pepper to taste.

4 Toss to coat all the ingredients in the olive oil and lemon, and to amalgamate the flavours.

5 If possible, allow the salad to stand for 10–15 minutes at room temperature before serving.

Cook's Tips
- *Feta cheese has a strong flavour and can be salty. The least salty variety is imported from Greece and Turkey.*
- *Wash and drain lamb's lettuce thoroughly before using as, like spinach, it can be quite gritty.*

Moroccan vegetable salad: Energy 269kcal/1115kJ; Protein 4g; Carbohydrate 18.7g, of which sugars 10.8g; Fat 20.3g, of which saturates 3.1g; Cholesterol 0mg; Calcium 99mg; Fibre 6.1g; Sodium 1705mg
Sun-ripened tomato & feta salad: Energy 283Kcal/1168kJ; Protein 7.2g; Carbohydrate 6.8g, of which sugars 6.3g; Fat 25.4g, of which saturates 7.7g; Cholesterol 26mg; Calcium 158mg; Fibre 1.9g; Sodium 717mg

Piquant Roasted Pepper Salad

This is the Moroccan cousin of gazpacho – roasting the peppers adds a sweet richness to the salad, which contrasts superbly with the tangy flavour of preserved lemons.

Serves 4
3 green (bell) peppers, quartered
4 large tomatoes
2 garlic cloves, finely chopped
30ml/2 tbsp olive oil
30ml/2 tbsp lemon juice
good pinch of paprika
pinch of ground cumin
¼ preserved lemon
salt and ground black pepper
fresh coriander (cilantro) and flat leaf parsley, to garnish

1 Grill (broil) the peppers skin-side up until the skins are blistered and charred. Place in a plastic bag and tie the ends. Leave for about 10 minutes, or until the peppers are cool enough to handle, then peel off the skins.

2 Cut the peppers into small pieces, discarding the seeds and core, and place in a serving dish.

3 Plunge the tomatoes into a pan of boiling water for about 30 seconds, then refresh in cold water. Peel off the skins and remove the seeds and cores. Chop coarsely and add to the peppers. Sprinkle the garlic on top and chill for 1 hour.

4 Blend together the olive oil, lemon juice, paprika and cumin and pour over the salad. Season with salt and pepper.

5 Rinse the preserved lemon in cold water and remove the flesh and pith. Cut the peel into slivers and sprinkle over the salad. Garnish with coriander and flat leaf parsley.

Cook's Tip
It is always better to use fresh, rather than bottled lemon juice; as a guide, 30ml/2 tbsp is the average yield from half a lemon.

Tomato, Bean & Fried Basil Salad

Various canned beans or chickpeas can be used instead of mixed beans in this simple dish, as they all taste good and make a wholesome and nutritious vegetarian salad.

Serves 4
15g/½oz/½ cup fresh basil
75ml/5 tbsp extra virgin olive oil
300g/11oz cherry tomatoes
400g/14oz can mixed beans, drained and rinsed
salt and ground black pepper

1 Reserve one-third of the basil leaves for garnish, then tear the remainder into pieces.

2 Pour the olive oil into a small pan. Add the torn basil and heat gently for 1 minute, until the basil sizzles and begins to colour.

3 Halve the cherry tomatoes and put them in a bowl with the mixed beans.

4 Pour in the basil oil and season with a little salt and plenty of freshly ground black pepper. Toss the ingredients together gently to coat.

5 Cover the salad and leave to marinate at room temperature for at least 30 minutes. Serve sprinkled with the reserved basil leaves.

Cook's Tips
- *Infusing basil in hot extra virgin olive oil brings out its wonderful, aromatic flavour, which works so well in almost any tomato dish.*
- *You can use any combination of canned beans or chickpeas in this salad.*
- *Choose vine-ripened cherry tomatoes for the best taste. They are widely available in supermarkets and more flavourful varieties are now becoming easier to find.*

Piquant roasted pepper salad: Energy 113kcal/469kJ; Protein 2.2g; Carbohydrate 12.3g, of which sugars 11.9g; Fat 6.4g, of which saturates 1g; Cholesterol 0mg; Calcium 19mg; Fibre 3.3g; Sodium 15mg
Tomato, bean & fried basil salad: Energy 404kcal/1701kJ; Protein 22.8g; Carbohydrate 46.5g, of which sugars 4.9g; Fat 15.4g, of which saturates 2.3g; Cholesterol 0mg; Calcium 113mg; Fibre 16.6g; Sodium 26mg

Roasted Peppers with Tomatoes

This Mediterranean-style dish is a real treat, whether you are a vegetarian or not. If you have time, make and dress this salad an hour or two before serving, as this will allow the juices to mingle and create the best mouthwatering salad.

Serves 4

1 red (bell) pepper
1 yellow (bell) pepper
4 ripe plum tomatoes, sliced
2 canned artichokes, drained and quartered
4 sun-dried tomatoes in oil, drained and thinly sliced
15ml/1 tbsp capers, drained
1 garlic clove, sliced

For the dressing

15ml/1 tbsp balsamic vinegar
5ml/1 tsp lemon juice
75ml/5 tbsp extra virgin olive oil
chopped fresh mixed herbs
salt and ground black pepper

1 Cut the peppers in half, and remove the seeds and stalks. Cut into quarters and place on a grill (broiler) pan covered with foil. Cook, skin-side up, under a grill set on high, until the skin chars. Transfer to a bowl and cover with crumpled kitchen paper. Leave the peppers to cool.

2 Rub the skin off the peppers, remove the seeds and cores, then cut into strips.

3 Arrange the pepper strips, fresh plum tomatoes and canned artichokes on a serving dish. Sprinkle over the sun-dried tomatoes, capers and garlic.

4 To make the dressing, put the balsamic vinegar and lemon juice in a bowl and whisk in the olive oil, then the chopped herbs. Season with salt and pepper. Pour the dressing over the salad 1–2 hours before the salad is served, if possible.

Variation
The flavour of the salad can be varied by using different herbs in the dressing. For a nutty flavour add a handful of pine nuts.

Fattoush

This simple salad has been served for centuries in the Middle East. A wonderful concoction of peppers, tomatoes, cucumber and fresh herbs, it makes a clean-tasting light meal.

Serves 4

1 yellow or red (bell) pepper, seeded and sliced
1 large cucumber, roughly chopped
4–5 tomatoes, chopped
1 bunch spring onions (scallions), sliced
30ml/2 tbsp finely chopped fresh parsley
30ml/2 tbsp finely chopped fresh mint
30ml/2 tbsp finely chopped fresh coriander (cilantro)
2 garlic cloves, crushed
juice of 1½ lemons
45ml/3 tbsp olive oil
salt and ground black pepper
2 pitta breads, to serve

1 Place the yellow or red pepper, cucumber and tomatoes in a large salad bowl. Add the spring onions, with the finely chopped parsley, mint and coriander.

2 To make the dressing, mix the garlic with the lemon juice in a bowl. Gradually whisk in the olive oil, then season to taste with salt and black pepper. Pour the dressing over the salad and toss lightly to mix.

3 Toast the pitta bread, in a toaster or under a hot grill (broiler) until crisp. Serve with the salad.

Cook's Tip
People either love or hate fresh coriander (cilantro). If you hate it, omit it and double the quantity of parsley.

Variations
If you prefer, make this salad in the traditional way – after toasting the pitta breads until crisp, crush them in your hand and sprinkle over the salad before serving.

Roasted peppers with tomatoes: Energy 216kcal/890kJ; Protein 1.5g; Carbohydrate 8.1g, of which sugars 7.9g; Fat 19.9g, of which saturates 2.9g; Cholesterol 0mg; Calcium 22mg; Fibre 2.4g; Sodium 24mg
Fattoush: Energy 120kcal/499kJ; Protein 2.4g; Carbohydrate 7.7g, of which sugars 7.5g; Fat 9.1g, of which saturates 1.4g; Cholesterol 0mg; Calcium 54mg; Fibre 3g; Sodium 18mg

Italian Roasted Pepper Salad

This is one of those lovely recipes that brings together perfectly the colours, flavours and textures of southern Italian food. It is best to serve this dish at room temperature.

Serves 4

3 red (bell) peppers
6 large plum tomatoes
2.5ml/½ tsp dried red chilli flakes
1 red onion, finely sliced
3 garlic cloves, finely chopped
grated rind and juice of 1 lemon
45ml/3 tbsp chopped fresh flat leaf parsley
30ml/2 tbsp extra virgin olive oil
salt
black and green olives and extra chopped flat leaf parsley, to garnish

1 Preheat the oven to 220°C/425°F/ Gas 7. Place the peppers on a baking sheet and roast for 10 minutes until the skins are slightly blackened.

2 Add the tomatoes to the baking sheet. Bake for 5 minutes more.

3 Place the charred peppers in a plastic bag. Close the top, trapping in the steam. Set the pepper aside, with the tomatoes, until they are cool.

4 Skin and seed the peppers. Chop the peppers and tomatoes roughly and place them both in a mixing bowl.

5 Add the chilli flakes, onion, garlic, lemon rind and juice. Sprinkle over the parsley. Mix the ingredients together, then transfer to a serving dish.

6 Season with salt, drizzle over the olive oil and sprinkle the olives and extra parsley over the top.

Cook's Tip

These peppers will keep for several weeks if the peeled pepper pieces are placed in a jar of olive oil, with a tight-fitting lid. Store in the refrigerator.

Date, Orange & Carrot Salad

A simple oil-free dressing is perfect on this juicy salad.

Serves 4

1 Little Gem (Bibb) lettuce
2 carrots, finely grated
2 oranges, segmented
115g/4oz/⅔ cup fresh dates, stoned (pitted) and sliced
30ml/2 tbsp toasted almonds
30ml/2 tbsp lemon juice
5ml/1 tsp caster (superfine) sugar
1.5ml/¼ tsp salt
15ml/1 tbsp orange flower water

1 Spread out the lettuce leaves on a platter. Place the carrot in the centre. Surround it with the oranges, dates and almonds.

2 Mix together the lemon juice, sugar, salt and orange flower water. Sprinkle over the salad and serve chilled.

Panzanella

Open-textured, Italian-style bread is essential for this colourful Tuscan salad.

Serves 6

10 thick slices day-old Italian-style bread, about 275g/10oz
1 cucumber, peeled and cut into chunks
5 tomatoes, seeded and diced
1 large red onion, chopped
175g/6oz/1½ cups pitted black or green olives
20 fresh basil leaves, torn

For the dressing

60ml/4 tbsp extra virgin olive oil
15ml/1 tbsp red or white wine vinegar
salt and ground black pepper

1 Soak the bread in water to cover for about 2 minutes, then lift it out and squeeze gently, first with your hands and then in a dish towel to remove any excess water.

2 Whisk the oil, vinegar and seasoning together. Mix the cucumber, tomatoes, onion and olives in a bowl.

3 Break the bread into chunks and add to the bowl with the basil. Pour the dressing over the salad, and toss before serving.

Italian roasted pepper salad: Energy 126kcal/527kJ; Protein 2.9g; Carbohydrate 14.6g, of which sugars 13.8g; Fat 6.6g, of which saturates 1.1g; Cholesterol 0mg; Calcium 49mg; Fibre 4.4g; Sodium 22mg
Date, orange & carrot salad: Energy 138kcal/582kJ; Protein 3.6g; Carbohydrate 21.8g, of which sugars 21.4g; Fat 4.7g, of which saturates 0.4g; Cholesterol 0mg; Calcium 90mg; Fibre 3.9g; Sodium 18mg
Panzanella: Energy 239kcal/1003kJ; Protein 5.5g; Carbohydrate 29.6g, of which sugars 7.1g; Fat 11.8g, of which saturates 1.6g; Cholesterol 0mg; Calcium 93mg; Fibre 3.3g; Sodium 905mg

Avocado, Tomato & Orange Salad

This salad has a feel of the Mediterranean – avocados are grown in many parts of the region and add a delicious flavour and texture to this dish. Take care to find avocados that are fully ripe, but not over-ripe.

Serves 4
2 oranges
4 well-flavoured tomatoes
2 small avocados
60ml/4 tbsp extra virgin olive oil
30ml/2 tbsp lemon juice
15ml/1 tbsp chopped fresh parsley
1 small onion, sliced into rings
salt and ground black pepper
25g/1oz/¼ cup flaked (sliced) almonds and olives, to garnish

1 Peel the oranges and slice into thick rounds. Plunge the tomatoes into boiling water for 30 seconds, then refresh in cold water. Peel off the skins, cut the tomatoes into quarters, remove the seeds and chop roughly.

2 Cut the avocados in half, remove the stones (pits) and carefully peel away the skin. Cut into chunks.

3 Whisk together the olive oil, lemon juice and parsley. Season with salt and pepper to taste. Toss the avocados and tomatoes in half the dressing.

4 Arrange the sliced oranges on a plate and scatter over the onion rings. Drizzle the remaining dressing over the oranges, then carefully spoon the avocados, tomatoes, almonds and olives on top of the salad.

Cook's Tip
Use avocados that are just ripe for this salad. They should yield to gentle pressure. Avoid any avocados with bruised areas, or that feel very soft. Unripe avocados will ripen in 4–7 days if stored at room temperature; they will ripen even sooner if you have bananas in the same bowl.

Nopalitos Salad

This unusual salad captures the authentic taste of Mexico. Nopalitos – strips of pickled cactus paddles – are sold in cans or jars, and are very useful for making quick and easy salads like this one.

Serves 4
300g/11oz/scant 2 cups drained canned nopalitos
1 red (bell) pepper
30ml/2 tbsp olive oil
2 garlic cloves, sliced
½ red onion, thinly sliced
120ml/4fl oz/½ cup cider vinegar
small bunch of fresh coriander (cilantro), chopped
salt

1 Preheat the grill (broiler). Put the nopalitos in a bowl. Pour over water to cover and set aside for 30 minutes. Drain the nopalitos, replace with fresh water and leave to soak for a further 30 minutes.

2 Place the red pepper halves cut-side down in a grill pan. Grill (broil) the peppers until the skins blister and char, then put the pepper halves in a strong plastic bag, tie the top securely to keep the steam in, and set aside for 20 minutes.

3 Heat the oil in a small frying pan and fry the garlic over a low heat until the slices start to turn golden. Using a slotted spoon, transfer them to a salad bowl. Pour the garlic-flavoured oil into a bowl and set it aside to cool.

4 Add the red onion slices to the salad bowl, then pour over the vinegar. Remove the red pepper from the bag, peel off the skins, then cut the flesh into thin strips. Add the peppers and onions to the salad bowl.

5 Drain the nopalitos thoroughly and add them to the salad, with the cooled garlic-flavoured oil and a little salt, to taste. Toss lightly, then chill until needed.

6 Sprinkle the chopped fresh coriander over the salad just before serving.

Avocado, tomato & orange salad: Energy 251kcal/1041kJ; Protein 2.7g; Carbohydrate 11.9g, of which sugars 10.9g; Fat 21.7g, of which saturates 3.8g; Cholesterol 0mg; Calcium 60mg; Fibre 4.3g; Sodium 155mg
Nopalitos salad: Energy 78kcal/325kJ; Protein 1.4g; Carbohydrate 5g, of which sugars 4.5g; Fat 6g, of which saturates 0.8g; Cholesterol 0mg; Calcium 63mg; Fibre 2.4g; Sodium 51mg

Italian Salad

A suberb combination of Italian antipasto ingredients and baked potato wedges makes this salad an extremely substantial vegetarian dish.

Serves 6

1 aubergine (eggplant), sliced
75ml/5 tbsp olive oil
2 garlic cloves, cut into slivers
4 sun-dried tomatoes in oil, halved
2 red (bell) peppers, halved, seeded and cut into large chunks
2 large baking potatoes, cut into wedges
10ml/2 tsp mixed dried Italian herbs
30–45ml/2–3 tbsp balsamic vinegar
salt and ground black pepper

1 Preheat the oven to 200°C/400°F/Gas 6. Place the aubergines in a medium roasting pan with the olive oil, garlic slivers and sun-dried tomatoes.

2 Lay the chunks of red pepper over the aubergines.

3 Arrange the potato wedges on top of the other ingredients in the roasting pan. Scatter the mixed herbs over and season with salt and black pepper.

4 Cover the pan with foil and bake in the preheated oven for 45 minutes.

5 Remove from the oven and turn the vegetables over. Then return to the oven and cook, uncovered, for a further 30 minutes.

6 Transfer the roasted vegetables to a serving dish using a slotted spoon.

7 Add the balsamic vinegar to the roasting pan, season with salt and ground black pepper, and whisk.

8 Pour over the vegetables. Season to taste with a little more salt and ground black pepper before serving.

Smoky Aubergine & Pepper Salad

Cooking the aubergines whole, over an open flame, gives them a distinctive smoky flavour and aroma, as well as tender, creamy flesh. The subtle flavour of the roasted aubergine contrasts wonderfully with the sweet flavour of the peppers.

Serves 4–6

2 aubergines (eggplants)
2 red (bell) peppers
3–5 garlic cloves, chopped, or more to taste
2.5ml/½ tsp ground cumin
juice of ½–1 lemon, to taste
2.5ml/½ tsp sherry or wine vinegar
45–60ml/3–4 tbsp extra virgin olive oil
1–2 shakes of cayenne pepper, Tabasco or other hot pepper sauce
coarse sea salt
chopped fresh coriander (cilantro), to garnish

To serve

pitta bread wedges or thinly sliced French bread or ciabatta bread
sesame seed crackers
cucumber slices

1 Place the aubergines and peppers directly over a medium-low gas flame or on the coals of a barbecue. Turn the vegetables frequently until the skins are blistered and charred.

2 Put the aubergines and peppers in a plastic bag or in a bowl and seal tightly. Leave to cool for about 30 minutes.

3 Peel the vegetables, reserving the juices, and roughly chop the flesh. Put the flesh in a bowl with the reserved juices.

4 Add the garlic, cumin, lemon juice, vinegar, olive oil, hot pepper seasoning and salt. Mix well to combine. Turn the mixture into a serving bowl and garnish with coriander. Serve with bread, sesame seed crackers and cucumber slices.

Cook's Tip

Shape and size are not important when choosing aubergines; the essentials are tight, glossy skins and a fairly firm texture.

Italian salad: Energy 154kcal/644kJ; Protein 2.2g; Carbohydrate 15.6g, of which sugars 3.1g; Fat 9.7g, of which saturates 1.5g; Cholesterol 0mg; Calcium 12mg; Fibre 2.2g; Sodium 17mg
Smoky aubergine & pepper salad: Energy 81kcal/335kJ; Protein 1.3g; Carbohydrate 5.6g, of which sugars 5.2g; Fat 6.1g, of which saturates 0.9g; Cholesterol 0mg; Calcium 13mg; Fibre 2.6g; Sodium 4mg

Lentil & Cabbage Salad

A warm, crunchy salad that makes a satisfying meal if served with crusty French bread or wholemeal rolls.

Serves 4–6

225g/8oz/1 cup Puy lentils
1.5 litres/2¼ pints/6¼ cups cold water
3 garlic cloves
1 bay leaf
1 small onion, peeled and studded with 2 cloves
15ml/1 tbsp olive oil
1 red onion, finely sliced
15ml/1 tbsp fresh thyme leaves
350g/12oz cabbage, finely shredded
finely grated rind and juice of 1 lemon
15ml/1 tbsp raspberry vinegar
salt and ground black pepper

1 Rinse the lentils in cold water and place in a large pan with the cold water, one of the garlic cloves, the bay leaf and clove-studded onion. Bring to the boil and cook for 10 minutes.

2 Reduce the heat, cover and simmer gently for 15–20 minutes. Drain and discard the onion, garlic and bay leaf.

3 Crush the remaining garlic cloves. Heat the oil in a large pan. Add the red onion, crushed garlic and thyme and cook for 5 minutes, until softened.

4 Add the cabbage and cook for 3–5 minutes, until just cooked but still crunchy. Stir in the cooked lentils, lemon rind and juice and the raspberry vinegar. Season with salt and black pepper to taste and serve warm.

Cook's Tip
The small, green Puy lentils, from France, have a fine flavour and are well worth using in this recipe.

Variation
Use spinach instead of cabbage; just cook briefly until wilted.

Ensaladilla

A Spanish version of what is commonly known as Russian salad, this dish is a meal in itself.

Serves 4

8 new potatoes, scrubbed and quartered
1 large carrot, diced
115g/4oz fine green beans, cut into 2cm/¾in lengths
75g/3oz/¾ cup peas
½ Spanish onion, chopped
4 cornichons or small gherkins, sliced
1 small red (bell) pepper, seeded and diced
50g/2oz/½ cup pitted black olives
15ml/1 tbsp drained pickled capers
15ml/1 tbsp freshly squeezed lemon juice
30ml/2 tbsp chopped fresh fennel or parsley
salt and ground black pepper

For the aïoli
2 garlic cloves, finely chopped
2.5ml/½ tsp salt
150ml/¼ pint/⅔ cup mayonnaise

1 To make the aïoli, crush the garlic with the salt in a mortar with a pestle, then whisk or stir into the mayonnaise.

2 Cook the potatoes and diced carrot in a pan of boiling lightly salted water for 5–8 minutes until almost tender.

3 Add the beans and peas to the pan and cook for 2 minutes, or until all the vegetables are tender. Drain well.

4 Transfer the vegetables to a large bowl. Add the onion, cornichons or gherkins, red pepper, olives and capers. Stir in the aïoli and season to taste with ground black pepper and lemon juice.

5 Toss the vegetables and aïoli together, adjust the seasoning and chill well. Serve garnished with fennel or parsley.

Variation
This salad is delicious using any combination of chopped, cooked vegetables. Use whatever is available.

Lentil & cabbage salad: Energy 155kcal/656kJ; Protein 9.9g; Carbohydrate 24.8g, of which sugars 4.3g; Fat 2.5g, of which saturates 0.3g; Cholesterol 0mg; Calcium 50mg; Fibre 3.2g; Sodium 18mg
Ensaladilla: Energy 397kcal/1645kJ; Protein 4.9g; Carbohydrate 25.3g, of which sugars 7.8g; Fat 31.4g, of which saturates 4.9g; Cholesterol 28mg; Calcium 47mg; Fibre 4.4g; Sodium 609mg

Caribbean Potato Salad

Colourful vegetables in a creamy smooth dressing make this piquant salad ideal to serve on its own or with a vegetable flan.

Serves 6

900g/2lb small waxy or salad potatoes
2 red (bell) peppers, seeded and diced
2 celery sticks, finely chopped
1 shallot, finely chopped
2 or 3 spring onions (scallions), finely chopped
1 mild fresh green chilli, seeded and finely chopped
1 garlic clove, crushed
10ml/2 tsp finely snipped chives
10ml/2 tsp finely chopped basil
15ml/1 tbsp finely chopped parsley
15ml/1 tbsp single (light) cream
30ml/2 tbsp salad cream
15ml/1 tbsp mayonnaise
5ml/1 tsp Dijon mustard
7.5ml/½ tbsp sugar
snipped chives and chopped red chilli, to garnish

1 Cook the potatoes in a large pan of boiling water until tender but still firm. Drain and set aside. When cool enough to handle, cut the potatoes into 2.5cm/1in cubes and place in a large salad bowl.

2 Add the peppers, celery, shallot and spring onions to the potatoes in the salad bowl, together with the chilli, garlic and all the chopped herbs.

3 Mix together the cream, salad cream, mayonnaise, mustard and sugar in a small bowl. Stir well until the mixture is thoroughly combined and forms a smooth dressing.

4 Pour the dressing over the potato mixture and stir gently to coat. Serve garnished with snipped chives and chopped red chilli.

Variation
To turn this salad into a more substantial meal-in-one, add quartered hard-boiled eggs and cooked green beans, serve on a bed of lettuce and top with sliced olives.

Pumpkin Salad

Red wine vinegar brings out the sweetness of the pumpkin in this tempting salad. No salad leaves are used, just plenty of fresh parsley. A great dish for serving at a cold buffet.

Serves 4

1 large red onion, peeled and very thinly sliced
200ml/7fl oz/scant 1 cup olive oil
60ml/4 tbsp red wine vinegar
675g/1½lb pumpkin, peeled and cut into 4cm/1½in pieces
40g/1½oz/¾ cup fresh flat leaf parsley leaves, chopped
salt and ground black pepper
fresh flat leaf parsley sprigs, to garnish (optional)

1 Mix the onion, olive oil and vinegar in a large bowl. Season with salt and ground black pepper, then stir well to combine.

2 Put the pumpkin pieces in a large pan of cold salted water. Bring to the boil, then lower the heat and simmer gently for 15–20 minutes. Drain.

3 Immediately add the drained pumpkin to the bowl containing the dressing and toss lightly with your hands. Leave to cool.

4 Stir in the chopped parsley, cover with clear film (plastic wrap) and chill until needed.

5 Allow the salad to come back to room temperature before serving. Garnish with fresh parsley sprigs, if you like.

Cook's Tip
The quality of red wine vinegar depends on the quality of the wine used to make it. The finest wine vinegars are costly, but add fabulous flavour to salad dressings.

Caribbean potato salad: Energy 176kcal/742kJ; Protein 3.8g; Carbohydrate 31.3g, of which sugars 8.7g; Fat 4.8g, of which saturates 1g; Cholesterol 5mg; Calcium 42mg; Fibre 3.2g; Sodium 92mg
Pumpkin salad: Energy 404kcal/1663kJ; Protein 1.7g; Carbohydrate 5.2g, of which sugars 4g; Fat 42g, of which saturates 6.1g; Cholesterol 0mg; Calcium 73mg; Fibre 2.4g; Sodium 4mg

Sweet & Sour Artichoke Salad

This Italian salad combines spring vegetables with a deliciously piquant sauce called agrodolce.

Serves 4

juice of 1 lemon
6 small globe artichokes
30ml/2 tbsp olive oil
2 medium onions, roughly chopped
175g/6oz/1 cup broad (fava) beans (shelled weight)
300ml/½ pint/1¼ cups water
175g/6oz/1½ cups fresh or frozen peas (shelled weight)
salt and ground black pepper
fresh mint leaves, to garnish

For the sauce

120ml/4fl oz/½ cup white wine vinegar
15ml/1 tbsp caster (superfine) sugar
a handful of fresh mint leaves, roughly torn

1 Fill a bowl with cold water and add the lemon juice. Pull off the outer leaves from the artichokes and discard them. Cut the artichokes into quarters and place them in the bowl of acidulated water to prevent them from discolouring.

2 Heat the oil in a large, heavy-based pan. Add the onions and fry over a low heat, stirring occasionally, until they are golden.

3 Stir in the beans, then drain the artichokes and add them to the pan. Pour in the measured water. Bring the water to the boil, lower the heat, cover and cook for 10–15 minutes.

4 Add the peas, season to taste with salt and pepper and cook for 5 minutes more, stirring from time to time, until the vegetables are tender. Drain thoroughly. Place in a bowl, leave to cool, then cover and chill.

5 To make the sauce, mix all the ingredients in a small pan. Heat gently for 2–3 minutes, until the sugar has dissolved. Simmer for about another 5 minutes, stirring occasionally. Remove from the heat and leave to cool.

6 To serve, drizzle the sauce over the vegetables and garnish with the fresh mint leaves.

Artichokes with Garlic & Lemon

With a lovely combination of simple ingredients, this salad really brings out the flavour of the artichokes.

Serves 4

4 globe artichokes
juice of 1–2 lemons, plus extra to acidulate water
60ml/4 tbsp extra-virgin olive oil
1 onion, chopped
5–8 garlic cloves, roughly chopped or thinly sliced
30ml/2 tbsp chopped fresh parsley
120ml/4fl oz/½ cup dry white wine
120ml/4fl oz/½ cup vegetable stock or water
salt and ground black pepper

1 To prepare the artichokes, trim the stalks of the artichokes close to the base, cut the very tips off the leaves and then divide them into quarters. Remove the inedible hairy choke (the central part), carefully scraping the hairs away from the heart at the base of the artichoke. Put in a bowl of water that has had lemon juice added to it.

2 Heat the oil in a pan, add the onion and garlic and fry for 5 minutes until softened. Stir in the parsley and cook for a few seconds. Add the wine, stock and drained artichokes. Season with half the lemon juice, salt and pepper.

3 Bring the mixture to the boil, then lower the heat, cover and simmer for 10–15 minutes until the artichokes are tender.

4 Lift out the artichokes using a slotted spoon and transfer them to a serving dish.

5 Bring the cooking liquid to the boil and boil until reduced to about half. Pour over the artichokes and drizzle over the remaining lemon juice. Adjust the seasoning. Cool before serving.

Cook's Tip

Placing trimmed artichokes in a bowl of water acidulated with lemon juice prevents them discolouring.

Sweet and sour artichoke salad: Energy 172kcal/717kJ; Protein 8g; Carbohydrate 21g, of which sugars 10.8g; Fat 6.8g, of which saturates 1g; Cholesterol 0mg; Calcium 106mg; Fibre 7.3g; Sodium 82mg
Artichokes with garlic & lemon: Energy 142kcal/586kJ; Protein 1.6g; Carbohydrate 4.1g, of which sugars 1.9g; Fat 11.3g, of which saturates 1.6g; Cholesterol 0mg; Calcium 40mg; Fibre 1.6g; Sodium 47mg

Pear & Pecan Nut Salad

Toasted pecan nuts have a special affinity with crisp white pears. Their robust flavours combine well with a rich cheese and chive dressing to make this a salad to remember.

Serves 4

75g/3oz/½ cup shelled pecan nuts, roughly chopped
3 crisp pears
1 escarole or round (butterhead) lettuce
1 radicchio
175g/6oz young spinach, stems removed
30ml/2 tbsp blue cheese and chive dressing
salt and ground black pepper
crusty bread, to serve

1 Toast the shelled pecan nuts under a medium grill (broiler) to bring out their flavour.

2 Cut the pears into even slices, leaving the skins intact but discarding the cores.

3 Separate the leaves on the lettuce and radicchio, then place in a large bowl with the spinach. Add the pear slices and toasted pecans.

4 Pour over the blue cheese dressing and toss well. Distribute among four large serving plates and season with salt and pepper. Serve the salad with warm crusty bread.

Cook's Tips

• *To make blue cheese and chive dip, add 50ml/2fl oz/¼ cup soured cream and 50g/2oz crumbled blue cheese to 75ml3fl oz/⅓ cup mayonnaise. Stir in a few drops of white wine vinegar, 15ml/1 tbsp snipped fresh chives and ground black pepper to taste. Beat well to combine.*

• *The pecan nuts will burn quickly under the grill, so watch them constantly and remove them as soon as they change colour.*

Chicory, Carrot & Rocket Salad in a Honey & Lemon dressing

A bright and colourful salad, which is ideal for a party. It looks stunning when arranged on the bed of chicory leaves.

Serves 4–6

3 carrots
about 50g/2oz fresh rocket (arugula) or watercress
1 large head chicory (Belgian endive)
Parmesan cheese, to garnish

For the dressing

45ml/3 tbsp sunflower oil
15ml/1 tbsp hazelnut or walnut oil (optional)
30ml/2 tbsp cider vinegar or wine vinegar
10ml/2 tsp clear honey
5ml/1 tsp grated lemon rind
15ml/1 tbsp poppy seeds
salt and ground black pepper

1 Coarsely grate the carrots and put in a large bowl.

2 Roughly chop the rocket or watercress and add to the bowl of carrots. Mix together and season well with salt and ground black pepper.

3 Put all the dressing ingredients in a screw-top jar, close the lid tightly and shake the jar vigorously to mix well.

4 Pour the dressing on to the carrots and green leaves. Toss the salad thoroughly.

5 Line a shallow salad bowl with the chicory leaves.

6 Spoon the salad into the centre of the chicory leaves. Chill in the refrigerator for 1 hour, then garnish with Parmesan shavings and serve.

Variation

Use watercress if you cannot obtain rocket.

Pear & pecan nut salad: Energy 233kcal/965kJ; Protein 4.2g; Carbohydrate 15.3g, of which sugars 14.9g; Fat 17.6g, of which saturates 1.2g; Cholesterol 3mg; Calcium 129mg; Fibre 5.1g; Sodium 151mg
Chicory, carrot & rocket salad: Energy 90kcal/374kJ; Protein 1.2g; Carbohydrate 5.2g, of which sugars 5g; Fat 7.3g, of which saturates 1g; Cholesterol 0mg; Calcium 51mg; Fibre 1.6g; Sodium 16mg

Courgette, Carrot & Pecan Salad

In this vegetarian lunch dish, hunks of warm fried courgettes are served with a crisp tangy salad in pockets of pitta bread.

Serves 2

2 carrots
25g/1oz/¼ cup pecan nuts
4 spring onions (scallions), sliced
50ml/2fl oz/¼ cup Greek (US strained plain) yogurt
35ml/7 tsp olive oil
5ml/1 tsp lemon juice
15ml/1 tbsp chopped fresh mint
2 courgettes (zucchini)
25g/1oz/¼ cup plain (all-purpose) flour
2 pitta breads
salt and ground black pepper
shredded lettuce, to serve

1 Coarsely grate the carrots into a bowl. Stir in the pecans and spring onions and toss well.

2 To make the dressing, whisk the yogurt with 7.5ml/1½ tsp of the olive oil, the lemon juice and the mint. Stir the dressing into the carrot mixture and mix well. Cover and chill until required.

3 Cut the courgettes diagonally into slices. Season the flour with salt and pepper. Spread it out on a plate and turn the courgette slices in it until they are well coated.

4 Heat the remaining oil in a large frying pan. Add the coated courgette slices and cook for 3–4 minutes, turning once, until browned. Drain the courgettes on kitchen paper.

5 Make a slit in each pitta bread to form a pocket. Fill the pittas with the carrot mixture and the courgette slices. Serve on a bed of shredded lettuce.

Cook's Tip
Warm the pitta breads in the oven or under a medium grill (broiler). Do not fill the pitta breads too soon or the carrot mixture will make the bread soggy.

Toasted Crottins with Beetroot Salad

Small goat's cheese rounds are grilled to a delicious, nutty creaminess in a matter of minutes for serving on thinly sliced walnut bread toast. A salad of grated raw beetroot, celery and spring onions makes a colourful accompaniment.

Serves 4

2 raw beetroots (beet), about 200g/7oz total weight
1 celery stick
2 spring onions (scallions)
60ml/4 tbsp French dressing
generous pinch of ground cumin
4 small slices of walnut bread
4 crottins (small goat's milk cheeses), about 60g/2¼oz each
a little butter, for spreading
salt and ground black pepper
rocket (arugula) or watercress leaves, to serve

1 Peel the beetroots and grate coarsely. Ideally, the beetroot should be served raw, but, if you prefer, blanch it in boiling water for 3 minutes, then drain, refresh under cold running water and drain again. Put the beetroot in a bowl.

2 Slice the celery and spring onions finely and toss with the beetroot, dressing and cumin. Add salt and pepper to taste. Leave to marinate for 1 hour or so, if possible, then mound onto four salad plates.

3 Preheat the grill (broiler). Toast the walnut bread lightly on each side. Keep warm.

4 Place a sheet of foil on the rack, add the crottins and grill (broil) for 3–5 minutes until they turn golden brown on top and just start to melt.

5 Meanwhile, butter the toast lightly. Place on the plates, then, using a palette knife, transfer the crottins to the toast and serve immediately, accompanied by the beetroot salad and rocket or watercress leaves.

Courgette, carrot & pecan salad: Energy 770kcal/3210kJ; Protein 14g; Carbohydrate 71.9g, of which sugars 9.7g; Fat 49.4g, of which saturates 6.6g; Cholesterol 0mg; Calcium 209mg; Fibre 5.8g; Sodium 455mg
Toasted crottins with beetroot salad: Energy 421kcal/1756kJ; Protein 18.2g; Carbohydrate 25.7g, of which sugars 6.1g; Fat 24.6g, of which saturates 12.9g; Cholesterol 58mg; Calcium 193mg; Fibre 2.9g; Sodium 775mg

Fruit & Raw Vegetable Gado-gado

A banana leaf, which can be bought from Asian stores, can be used instead of the mixed salad leaves to line the platter for a special occasion.

Serves 6

½ cucumber
2 pears (not too ripe) or 175g/6oz wedge of yam bean
1–2 eating apples
juice of ½ lemon
mixed salad leaves
6 small tomatoes, cut in wedges
3 slices fresh pineapple, cored and cut in wedges
3 eggs, hard-boiled and shelled
175g/6oz egg noodles, cooked, cooled and chopped
deep-fried onions, to garnish

For the peanut sauce

2–4 fresh red chillies, seeded and ground, or 15ml/1 tbsp chilli sambal
300ml/½ pint/1¼ cups coconut milk
350g/12oz/1¼ cups crunchy peanut butter
15ml/1 tbsp dark soy sauce or dark brown sugar
5ml/1 tsp tamarind pulp, soaked in 45ml/3 tbsp warm water
coarsely crushed peanuts
salt

1 To make the peanut sauce, put the ground chillies or chilli sambal in a pan. Pour in the coconut milk, then stir in the peanut butter. Heat gently, stirring constantly, until the ingredients are well blended.

2 Simmer gently until the sauce thickens, then stir in the soy sauce or sugar. Strain in the tamarind juice, add salt to taste and stir well. Spoon into a small serving bowl and sprinkle with a few coarsely crushed peanuts.

3 To make the salad, core the cucumber and peel the pears or yam bean. Cut them into matchsticks. Finely shred the apples and sprinkle them with the lemon juice.

4 Spread a bed of lettuce leaves on a flat platter, then pile the fruit and vegetables on top.

5 Add the sliced or quartered hard-boiled eggs, the chopped noodles and the deep-fried onions. Serve immediately, with the peanut sauce.

Gado-gado Salad with Peanut Sambal

This classic Indonesian salad combines lightly steamed vegetables and hard-boiled eggs with a richly flavoured peanut dressing.

Serves 6

225g/8oz new potatoes, halved
2 carrots, cut into sticks
115g/4oz green beans
½ small cauliflower, broken into florets
¼ firm white cabbage, shredded
200g/7oz bean or lentil sprouts
4 eggs, hard-boiled and quartered
bunch of watercress (optional)

For the sauce

90ml/6 tbsp crunchy peanut butter
300ml/½ pint/1¼ cups cold water
1 garlic clove, crushed
30ml/2 tbsp dark soy sauce
15ml/1 tbsp dry sherry
10ml/2 tsp caster (superfine) sugar
15ml/1 tbsp fresh lemon juice

1 Place the halved new potatoes in a metal colander or steamer and set over a pan of gently boiling water. Cover the pan or steamer with a lid and cook the potatoes for 10 minutes.

2 Add the rest of the vegetables to the steamer and steam for a further 10 minutes, until tender.

3 Cool the potatoes and vegetables and arrange on a platter with the egg quarters and the watercress, if using.

4 Beat together all the ingredients for the sauce in a large mixing bowl until smooth.

5 Drizzle a little sauce over the salad then pour the rest into a small bowl and serve separately.

Variation

There are a range of nut butters available in supermarkets and health-food stores. Try using hazelnut, almond or cashew nut butter in place of peanut butter to create a milder sauce.

Raw vegetable gado-gado: Energy 495kcal/2066kJ; Protein 18.7g; Carbohydrate 30.8g, of which sugars 23.3g; Fat 34g, of which saturates 8.5g; Cholesterol 97mg; Calcium 91mg; Fibre 6.9g; Sodium 489mg
Gado-gado salad: Energy 199kcal/831kJ; Protein 10.5g; Carbohydrate 14g, of which sugars 6.6g; Fat 11.3g, of which saturates 2.9g; Cholesterol 127mg; Calcium 58mg; Fibre 3.1g; Sodium 819mg

Green Papaya Salad

This salad appears in many guises in South-east Asia. As green (or unripe) papaya is not easy to get hold of, finely grated carrots, cucumber or green apple can be used instead. Alternatively, use very thinly sliced white cabbage.

Serves 4

1 green papaya
4 garlic cloves, roughly chopped
15ml/1 tbsp chopped shallots
3–4 fresh red chillies, seeded and sliced
2.5ml/½ tsp salt
2–3 snake beans or 6 green beans, cut into 2cm/¾in lengths
2 tomatoes, cut into thin wedges
45ml/3 tbsp light soy sauce
15ml/1 tbsp caster (superfine) sugar
juice of 1 lime
30ml/2 tbsp crushed roasted peanuts
sliced fresh red chillies, to garnish

1 Cut the papaya in half lengthwise. Scrape out the seeds with a spoon, then remove the peel using a swivel vegetable peeler or a small sharp knife. Grate the flesh finely using a food processor or grater.

2 Put the garlic, shallots, chillies and salt in a large mortar and grind to a paste using a pestle.

3 Add the grated papaya, a little at a time, pounding until it becomes slightly limp and soft.

4 Add the sliced beans and wedges of tomato to the mortar and crush them lightly with the pestle.

5 Season the mixture with soy sauce, sugar and lime juice. Transfer the salad to a serving dish, sprinkle with crushed peanuts and garnish with sliced red chillies.

Cook's Tip
Snake beans are extremely long, green, stringless beans. They are available from Oriental stores.

Bamboo Shoot Salad

This hot, sharp-flavoured salad originated in north-eastern Thailand. Use canned whole bamboo shoots, if you can find them – they have more flavour than sliced ones. This salad is great served with noodles and stir-fried vegetables.

Serves 4

400g/14oz canned bamboo shoots, in large pieces
25g/1oz/about 3 tbsp glutinous rice
30ml/2 tbsp chopped shallots
15ml/1 tbsp chopped garlic
45ml/3 tbsp chopped spring onions (scallions)
30ml/2 tbsp light soy sauce
30ml/2 tbsp fresh lime juice
5ml/1 tsp sugar
2.5ml/½ tsp dried chilli flakes
20–25 small fresh mint leaves
15ml/1 tbsp toasted sesame seeds

1 Rinse the bamboo shoots under cold running water, then drain them and pat them thoroughly dry with kitchen paper and set them aside.

2 Dry-roast the rice in a frying pan until it is golden brown. Leave to cool slightly.

3 Turn the rice into a mortar. Grind to fine crumbs with a pestle.

4 Transfer the rice to a bowl and add the shallots, garlic, spring onions, soy sauce, lime juice, sugar, chillies and half the mint leaves. Mix well.

5 Add the bamboo shoots to the bowl and toss to mix.

6 Serve sprinkled with the toasted sesame seeds and the remaining fresh mint leaves.

Cook's Tip
Glutinous rice does not, in fact, contain any gluten – it's just sticky. It is very popular in South-east Asian cooking.

Green papaya salad: Energy 109kcal/461kJ; Protein 3.4g; Carbohydrate 16.5g, of which sugars 15.9g; Fat 3.8g, of which saturates 0.7g; Cholesterol 0mg; Calcium 40mg; Fibre 3.5g; Sodium 811mg
Bamboo shoot salad: Energy 72kcal/305kJ; Protein 3.9g; Carbohydrate 13g, of which sugars 6.2g; Fat 0.7g, of which saturates 0.1g; Cholesterol 0mg; Calcium 31mg; Fibre 1.9g; Sodium 185mg

Salad Rolls with Pumpkin, Tofu, Peanuts & Basil

This is a type of 'do-it-yourself' dish. You place all the ingredients on the table with the rice wrappers for everyone to assemble their own rolls.

Serves 4–5

about 30ml/2 tbsp groundnut (peanut) or sesame oil
175g/6oz tofu, rinsed and patted dry
4 shallots, halved and sliced
2 garlic cloves, finely chopped
350g/12oz pumpkin flesh, cut into strips
1 carrot, cut into strips
15ml/1 tbsp soy sauce
120ml/4fl oz/½ cup water
3–4 green Thai chillies, seeded and finely sliced
1 small, crispy lettuce, torn into strips
1 bunch fresh basil, stalks removed
115g/4oz/⅔ cup roasted peanuts, chopped
100ml/3½fl oz/scant ½ cup hoisin sauce
20 dried rice wrappers
salt

1 Heat a heavy pan and smear with a little oil. Place the block of tofu in the pan and sear on both sides. Transfer to a plate and cut into thin strips.

2 Heat 30ml/2 tbsp oil in the pan and stir in the shallots and garlic. Add the pumpkin and carrot, then pour in the soy sauce and the water. Add a little salt to taste and cook gently until the vegetables have softened but still have a bite to them.

3 Meanwhile, arrange the tofu, chillies, lettuce, basil, peanuts and hoisin sauce in separate dishes and put them on the table. Provide a small bowl of hot water for each person, and place the stack of rice wrappers beside each. Turn the cooked vegetable mixture into a dish and add to the bowls of ingredients on the table.

4 To eat, take a rice wrapper and dip it in hot water for a few seconds to soften. Lay the wrapper flat and layer a little of each ingredient in a neat stack on top. Roll up the wrapper to eat.

Japanese Salad

Delicate and refreshing, this combines a mild-flavoured, sweet-tasting seaweed with crisp radishes, cucumber and beansprouts.

Serves 4

15g/½oz/ ½ cup dried hijiki
250g/9oz/1¼ cups radishes, sliced into very thin rounds
1 small cucumber, cut into thin sticks
75g/3oz/¾ cup beansprouts

For the dressing

15ml/1 tbsp sunflower oil
15ml/1 tbsp toasted sesame oil
5ml/1 tsp light soy sauce
30ml/2 tbsp rice vinegar or 15ml/1 tbsp wine vinegar
15ml/1 tbsp mirin or dry sherry

1 Place the hijiki in a bowl and add cold water to cover. Soak for 10–15 minutes, until it is rehydrated, then drain, rinse under cold running water and drain again. It should have almost trebled in volume.

2 Place the hijiki in a pan of water. Bring to the boil, then lower the heat and simmer for about 30 minutes, or until tender. Drain thoroughly.

3 Meanwhile, make the dressing. Place the sunflower and sesame oils, soy sauce, vinegar and mirin or sherry in a screw-top jar. Shake vigorously to combine.

4 Arrange the hijiki in a shallow bowl or platter with the radishes, cucumber and beansprouts. Pour the dressing over the salad and toss lightly.

Cook's Tip

Hijiki is a type of seaweed. A rich source of minerals, it comes from Japan, where it has a distinguished reputation for enhancing beauty and adding lustre to hair. Look for hijiki in Oriental food stores.

Salad rolls: Energy 312kcal/1300kJ; Protein 11.2g; Carbohydrate 28.9g, of which sugars 10.4g; Fat 16.9g, of which saturates 2.9g; Cholesterol 0mg; Calcium 231mg; Fibre 3.3g; Sodium 547mg
Japanese salad: Energy 68Kcal/280kJ; Protein 1.4g; Carbohydrate 2.8g, of which sugars 2.4g; fat 5.8g, of which saturates 0.8g; Cholesterol 0mg; Calcium 23mg; Fibre 1.1g; Sodium 276mg

Cambodian Soya Beansprout Salad with Spring Onions

Unlike mung beansprouts, soya beansprouts are slightly poisonous raw and need to be par-boiled before using. Tossed in a salad and served with noodles and rice they make a perfect light meal.

Serves 4

450g/1lb fresh soya beansprouts
2 spring onions (scallions), finely sliced
1 small bunch fresh coriander (cilantro), stalks removed

For the dressing

15ml/1 tbsp sesame oil
30ml/2tbsp light soy sauce
15ml/1 tbsp white rice vinegar
10ml/2 tsp palm sugar (jaggery)
1 fresh red chilli, seeded and finely sliced
15g/½ oz fresh young root ginger, finely shredded

1 To make the dressing, put the sesame oil, soy sauce and rice vinegar in a bowl with the palm sugar, and beat until the sugar dissolves. Stir in the sliced chilli and shredded ginger and leave to stand for 30 minutes.

2 Bring a pan of salted water to the boil. Drop in the beansprouts and blanch for a minute only.

3 Drain the beansprouts and refresh them under cold water until cool. Drain again and put them into a clean dish towel. Shake out the excess water.

4 Put the beansprouts into a bowl with the spring onions. Pour over the dressing and toss well. Garnish with coriander leaves and serve immediately.

Cook's Tip

Look for firm pieces of fresh root ginger, with smooth skin. If bought really fresh, it will keep for 2 weeks in a cool place.

Raw Vegetable Yam

In Thai cooking, 'yam' dishes are salads made with raw or lightly cooked vegetables, dressed with a special spicy sauce. They are a real treat.

Serves 4

50g/2oz watercress or baby spinach, chopped
½ cucumber, finely diced
2 celery sticks, finely diced
2 carrots, finely diced
1 red (bell) pepper, seeded and finely diced
2 tomatoes, seeded and finely diced
small bunch fresh mint, chopped
90g/3½oz cellophane noodles

For the yam

2 small fresh red chillies, seeded and finely chopped
60ml/4 tbsp light soy sauce
45ml/3 tbsp lemon juice
5ml/1 tsp palm sugar (jaggery) or light muscovado (brown) sugar
60ml/4 tbsp water
1 head pickled garlic, finely chopped, plus 15ml/1 tbsp vinegar from the jar
50g/2oz/scant ½ cup peanuts, roasted and chopped
90g/3½oz fried tofu, finely chopped
15ml/1 tbsp sesame seeds, toasted

1 Place the watercress or spinach, cucumber, celery, carrots, red pepper and tomatoes in to a serving bowl. Add the chopped mint and toss everything together.

2 Soak the cellophane noodles in boiling water for 3 minutes, or according to the packet instructions, then drain well and snip them into shorter lengths using scissors. Add them to the vegetables.

3 To make the yam, put the chopped chillies in a pan and add the soy sauce, lemon juice, sugar and water. Place over a medium heat and stir until the sugar has dissolved.

4 Add the chopped pickled garlic, with the pickling vinegar from the jar, then mix in the chopped nuts, tofu and toasted sesame seeds.

5 Pour the yam over the vegetables and noodles, toss together until well mixed, and serve immediately.

Cambodian soya beansprout salad: Energy 95kcal/396kJ; Protein 4.5g; Carbohydrate 8.4g, of which sugars 5.6g; Fat 5.6g, of which saturates 0.5g; Cholesterol 3mg; Calcium 54mg; Fibre 2.4g; Sodium 79mg
Raw vegetable yam: Energy 276kcal/1152kJ; Protein 12.1g; Carbohydrate 28.8g, of which sugars 9g; Fat 12.4g, of which saturates 1.5g; Cholesterol 0mg; Calcium 415mg; Fibre 3.1g; Sodium 1101mg

Tomato & Feta Cheese Salad with Black Olives

Sweet, sun-ripened tomatoes are rarely more delicious than when served with feta cheese and olive oil. Serve with warm pitta bread to complete the Greek character of the dish.

Serves 4
900g/2lb tomatoes
200g/7oz feta cheese
120ml/4fl oz/½ cup olive oil
12 black olives
4 fresh basil sprigs
ground black pepper

1 Remove any tough cores from the tomatoes, using a small, sharp knife.

2 Slice the tomatoes thickly and arrange them attractively in a shallow serving dish.

3 Crumble the feta cheese over the tomatoes and sprinkle with the olive oil.

4 Scatter the black olives and basil sprigs over the salad and season to taste with black pepper.

5 Serve the salad at room temperature.

Cook's Tips

- *Feta cheese has a strong flavour and can be salty. The least salty variety is imported from Greece and Turkey.*
- *Like feta cheese, olives are often salty so you will not need to add salt to this salad. Simply season to taste with ground black pepper.*
- *Tomatoes are tastiest when left to ripen on the vine, so try to buy 'vine-ripened' varieties. These are now widely available in supermarkets.*
- *Use a serrated knife to slice the tomatoes. If you use a flat-edged knife, make sure it is very sharp to prevent squashing or bruising the fruit.*

Broad Bean & Feta Salad

This recipe is loosely based on a typical medley of fresh-tasting Greek salad ingredients – broad beans, tomatoes and feta cheese. It is lovely as an appetizer, served warm or cold and accompanied by pitta bread.

Serves 4–6
900g/2lb broad (fava) beans, shelled, or 350g/12oz shelled frozen beans
60ml/4 tbsp olive oil
175g/6oz plum tomatoes, halved, or quartered if large
4 garlic cloves, crushed
115g/4oz/1 cup firm feta cheese, cut into chunks
45ml/3 tbsp chopped fresh dill
12 black olives
salt and ground black pepper
chopped fresh dill, to garnish

1 Cook the fresh or frozen broad beans in boiling, salted water until just tender. Drain and set aside.

2 Meanwhile, heat the oil in a heavy-based frying pan and add the tomatoes and crushed garlic. Cook until the tomatoes are beginning to colour.

3 Add the feta cheese to the pan and toss the ingredients together for 1 minute.

4 Mix with the drained beans, chopped dill, and black olives.

5 Season with salt and ground black pepper to taste and serve garnished with chopped dill.

Cook's Tip

When buying broad beans in their pods, look for bright-green, smooth, plump pods. Store them in the refrigerator for no more than 1–2 days before using.

Tomato & feta salad: Energy 369kcal/1528kJ; Protein 9.6g; Carbohydrate 7.7g, of which sugars 7.7g; Fat 33.5g, of which saturates 10.4g; Cholesterol 35mg; Calcium 211mg; Fibre 3g; Sodium 1303mg
Broad bean & feta salad: Energy 175kcal/727kJ; Protein 8.3g; Carbohydrate 8.8g, of which sugars 2.2g; Fat 12g, of which saturates 3.8g; Cholesterol 13mg; Calcium 121mg; Fibre 4.7g; Sodium 342mg

Watermelon & Feta Salad with Mixed Seeds & Olives

The combination of sweet watermelon with salty feta cheese is refreshing and flavoursome. The salad may be served plain and light, on a leafy base, or with a herbed dressing drizzled over. It is perfect served as an appetizer or as part of a summery mezze spread.

Serves 4

4 slices watermelon, chilled
130g/4½ oz feta cheese, preferably sheep's milk feta, cut into bitesize pieces
handful of mixed seeds, such as pumpkin seeds and sunflower seeds, lightly toasted
10–15 black olives

1 Using a sharp knife, cut the rind off the watermelon and remove and discard as many seeds as possible. The sweetest and juiciest part of the melon is right in the core. You may want to cut off any whiter flesh just under the skin.

2 Cut the flesh into triangular chunks and place in a salad bowl. Add the feta cheese, mixed seeds and black olives and mix gently to combine.

3 Cover and chill the salad for 30 minutes before serving.

Cook's Tips

- *Choose a watermelon that is firm and unbruised with no soft spots. It should feel quite heavy for its size and sound hollow when you tap it.*
- *Store the watermelon in the refrigerator for up to 1 week or 4 days in a cool, dark place.*
- *Once the melon is cut, wrap it in clear film (plastic wrap) and store in the refrigerator for up to 3 days.*
- *Watermelon is best served chilled, so keep it in the refrigerator until you are ready to use it.*
- *Watermelon contains the powerful antioxidants vitamin C and vitamin A.*

Rocket, Pear & Parmesan Salad

For a sophisticated start to an elaborate meal, try this simple salad of honey-rich pears, fresh Parmesan and aromatic rocket leaves.

Serves 4

3 ripe pears, such as Williams or Packhams
10ml/2 tsp lemon juice
45ml/3 tbsp hazelnut or walnut oil
115g/4oz rocket (arugula) leaves
75g/3oz piece Parmesan cheese
ground black pepper

1 Peel and core the pears and slice thickly. Moisten with lemon juice to keep the flesh white.

2 Combine the hazelnut or walnut oil with the pears. Add the rocket leaves and toss together.

3 Turn the salad out on to four individual plates and top with shavings of Parmesan cheese.

4 Season with ground black pepper and serve.

Cook's Tips

- *Buy a chunk of fresh Parmesan cheese and shave strips off the side, using a vegetable peeler. The distinctive flavour is quite strong. Store the rest of the Parmesan cheese, uncovered, in the refrigerator.*
- *Moistening the pears with lemon juice will prevent them from discolouring once the flesh is in contact with the air. You can also use lime juice.*
- *Pears are great in both sweet and savoury dishes and there are many different varieties: Williams pears have thin yellow skin and sweet, soft flesh and Packhams pears have creamy white flesh, a smooth texture and are very juicy. They both hold their shape well so are perfect for tossing in a salad. When ripe, they will yield to gentle pressure at the stem end.*

Watermelon & feta salad: Energy 203Kcal/849kJ; Protein 7.8g; Carbohydrate 16.2g, of which sugars 14.8g; Fat 12.4g, of which saturates 5.2g; Cholesterol 23mg; Calcium 148mg; Fibre 1.1g; Sodium 754mg
Rocket, pear & parmesan salad: Energy 210kcal/875kJ; Protein 8.6g; Carbohydrate 11.4g, of which sugars 11.4g; Fat 14.8g, of which saturates 4.7g; Cholesterol 19mg; Calcium 286mg; Fibre 2.9g; Sodium 222mg

Pear & Blue Cheese Salad

This salad is very quick to assemble, making it just the thing for an impromptu gathering. The key to success is to use pears that are just ripe and a blue cheese with lots of bite.

Serves 4
4 ripe pears
115g/4oz blue cheese
15ml/1 tbsp balsamic vinegar
30ml/2 tbsp olive oil
salt and ground black pepper

1 Cut the pears into quarters and remove the cores.

2 Thinly slice each pear quarter and arrange the slices on a serving platter.

3 Cut the blue cheese into bitesize pieces, or crumble roughly, and scatter over the pears.

4 Whisk the balsamic vinegar and olive oil together and drizzle over the pears.

5 Season with salt and ground black pepper, and serve.

Cook's Tips

• *Rich, dark balsamic vinegar has an intense yet mellow flavour. It is produced in Modena in the north of Italy and is widely available in most supermarkets. You could use wine vinegar instead, if you like.*
• *A mature Stilton, with it slightly crumbly texture, would make an excellent choice for this dish. Look for a piece where the veins of blue are evenly spread throughout the cheese. Other suitable cheeses would be Roquefort or Gorgonzola.*
• *Check that the pears are ripe by pressing them at the stalk end. They should yield to gentle pressure.*
• *If you are preparing the pears in advance, rub them with a little lemon juice to prevent them from discolouring.*
• *There are many varieties of pears to choose from, for example, Williams, Packhams or Comice.*

Watercress Salad with Pear & Dunsyre Blue Dressing

A refreshing light salad, this starter combines lovely peppery watercress, soft juicy pears and a tart dressing. Dunsyre Blue has a wonderfully sharp flavour with a crumbly texture.

Serves 4
25g/1oz Dunsyre Blue cheese
30ml/2 tbsp walnut oil
15ml/1 tbsp lemon juice
2 bunches watercress, thoroughly washed and trimmed
2 ripe pears
salt and ground black pepper

1 Crumble the Dunsyre Blue into a bowl, then mash into the walnut oil, using a fork.

2 Whisk in the lemon juice to create a thickish mixture. If you need to thicken it further, add a little more cheese. Season to taste with salt and ground black pepper.

3 Arrange a pile of watercress on the side of four plates.

4 Peel and slice the two pears then place the pear slices to the side of the watercress, allowing half a pear per person. You can also put the pear slices on top of the watercress, if you prefer. Drizzle the dressing over the salad. The salad is best served immediately at room temperature.

Cook's Tips

• *Choose ripe Comice or similar pears that are soft and juicy.*
• *If you want to get things ready in advance, peel and slice the pears then rub with some lemon juice; this will stop them discolouring so quickly.*

Variation

For a milder, tangy dressing use Dolcelatte cheese instead.

Pear & blue cheese salad: Energy 208kcal/865kJ; Protein 6.4g; Carbohydrate 15g, of which sugars 15g; Fat 14g, of which saturates 6.3g; Cholesterol 22mg; Calcium 157mg; Fibre 3.3g; Sodium 355mg
Watercress salad: Energy 106Kcal/442kJ; Protein 2.3g; Carbohydrate 7.6g, of which sugars 7.6g; Fat 7.6g, of which saturates 1.8g; Cholesterol 5mg; Calcium 81mg; Fibre 2g; Sodium 91mg

Goat's Cheese & Fig Salad

Fresh figs and walnuts, goat's cheese and couscous make a tasty salad, full of texture. The dressing has no vinegar, depending instead on the acidity of the goat's cheese.

Serves 4

175g/6oz/1 cup couscous
30ml/2 tbsp toasted buckwheat
1 egg, hard-boiled
30ml/2 tbsp chopped parsley
60ml/4 tbsp olive oil
45ml/3 tbsp walnut oil
115g/4oz rocket (arugula) leaves
½ frisée lettuce
175g/6oz crumbly white goat's cheese
50g/2oz/½ cup broken walnuts, toasted
4 ripe figs, trimmed and almost cut into four (leave the pieces joined at the base)

1 Place the couscous and toasted buckwheat in a bowl, cover with boiling water and leave to soak for 15 minutes. Place in a strainer to drain off any remaining water, then spread out on a metal tray and allow to cool.

2 Shell the hard-boiled egg and grate finely. Toss the grated egg, parsley, couscous and buckwheat together in a bowl.

3 Combine the olive and walnut oils and use half to moisten the couscous mixture.

4 Toss the rocket and lettuce in the remaining olive oil and distribute evenly between four large serving plates. Pile the couscous mixture into the centre of each plate and then crumble the goat's cheese over the top. Scatter with toasted walnuts, place a fig in the centre of each plate and serve the salad immediately.

Cook's Tip
Goat's cheeses vary in strength from the youngest, which are soft and mild, to strongly-flavoured, mature cheeses, which have a firm and crumbly texture. The crumbly varieties are best suited to salads.

Goat's Cheese Salad with Hazelnut Dressing

A herb-flavoured salad tossed with crunchy, toasted hazelnuts and topped with fresh-tasting goat's cheese makes a delightful lunch dish. Serve the salad with crusty French-style bread or Melba toast.

Serves 4

175g/6oz mixed salad leaves, such as lamb's lettuce, rocket (arugula), radicchio, frisée or cress
a few fresh large-leaf herbs, such as chervil and flat leaf parsley
15ml/1 tbsp toasted hazelnuts, roughly chopped
15–20 goat's cheese balls or cubes

For the dressing
30ml/2 tbsp hazelnut oil, olive oil or sunflower oil
5–10ml/1–2 tsp sherry vinegar or good wine vinegar, to taste
salt and ground black pepper

1 Tear up any large salad leaves. Put all the leaves into a large salad bowl with the fresh herbs and most of the toasted, chopped nuts (reserve a few for the garnish).

2 To make the dressing, whisk the hazelnut, olive or sunflower oil and vinegar together, and then season with salt and pepper.

3 Just before serving, toss the salad in the dressing and divide it among four serving plates. Arrange the drained goat's cheese on the leaves and sprinkle over the remaining chopped nuts.

Cook's Tip
A grilled (broiled) slice from a goat's cheese log can replace the cheese balls or cubes, just to ring the changes.

Variation
Toasted flaked (sliced) almonds could replace the hazelnuts, teamed with extra virgin olive oil.

Goat's cheese & fig salad: Energy 581kcal/2410kJ; Protein 17g; Carbohydrate 35.9g, of which sugars 13.3g; Fat 41.9g, of which saturates 11.4g; Cholesterol 88mg; Calcium 189mg; Fibre 3.5g; Sodium 301mg
Goat's cheese salad: Energy 225kcal/931kJ; Protein 11g; Carbohydrate 1.4g, of which sugars 1.3g; Fat 19.5g, of which saturates 8.7g; Cholesterol 41mg; Calcium 138mg; Fibre 1.2g; Sodium 325mg

Grilled Halloumi & Bean Salad with Skewered Potatoes

Halloumi, the hard, white salty goat's milk cheese that squeaks when you bite it, grills really well and is the perfect complement to fresh-tasting vegetables.

Serves 4

20 baby new potatoes, total weight about 300g/11oz
200g/7oz extra-fine green beans, trimmed
675g/1½lb broad (fava) beans, shelled weight 225g/8oz
200g/7oz halloumi cheese, cut into 5mm/¼in slices
1 garlic clove, crushed to a paste with a large pinch of salt
90ml/6 tbsp olive oil
5ml/1 tsp cider vinegar or white wine vinegar
15g/½oz/½ cup fresh basil leaves, shredded
45ml/3 tbsp chopped fresh savory
2 spring onions (scallions), finely sliced
salt and ground black pepper

1 Thread five potatoes onto each skewer, and cook in a large pan of salted boiling water for about 7 minutes or until almost tender. Add the green beans and cook for 3 minutes more. Add the broad beans and cook for just 2 minutes. Drain all the vegetables in a large colander.

2 Refresh the cooked broad beans under cold water. Pop each broad bean out its skin to reveal the bright green inner bean. Place in a bowl, cover and set aside.

3 Preheat a grill (broiler) or griddle. Place the halloumi slices and the potato skewers in a wide dish. Whisk the garlic and oil together with a generous grinding of black pepper. Add to the dish and toss the halloumi and potato skewers in the mixture.

4 Cook the cheese and potato skewers under the grill or on the griddle for about 2 minutes on each side.

5 Add the vinegar to the oil and garlic remaining in the dish and whisk to mix. Toss in the beans, herbs and spring onions, with the cooked halloumi. Serve with the potato skewers.

Salad of Roasted Shallots & Butternut Squash with Feta Cheese

This is especially good served with a grain or starchy salad, based on rice or couscous, for example. Serve with plenty of good bread to mop up the juices.

Serves 4–6

75ml/5 tbsp olive oil
15ml/1 tbsp balsamic vinegar, plus a little extra to taste
15ml/1 tbsp sweet soy sauce
350g/12oz shallots, peeled but left whole
3 fresh red chillies
1 butternut squash, peeled, seeded and cut into chunks
5ml/1 tsp finely chopped fresh thyme
15g/½oz flat leaf parsley
1 small garlic clove, finely chopped
75g/3oz walnuts, chopped
150g/5oz feta cheese
salt and ground black pepper

1 Preheat the oven to 200°C/400°F/Gas 6. Beat the oil, vinegar and soy sauce together in a large bowl, then season with salt and pepper.

2 Toss the shallots and two of the chillies in the oil mixture and turn into a large roasting pan or ovenproof dish. Roast for 15 minutes, stirring once or twice.

3 Add the butternut squash and roast for 30–35 minutes more, stirring once, until the squash is tender and browned.

4 Remove from the oven, stir in the chopped thyme and set the vegetables aside to cool.

5 Chop the parsley and garlic together and mix with the walnuts. Seed and finely chop the remaining chilli.

6 Stir the parsley, garlic and walnut mixture into the vegetables. Add chopped chilli to taste and adjust the seasoning, adding a little extra balsamic vinegar to taste.

7 Crumble the feta and add to the salad. Transfer to a serving dish and serve immediately.

Halloumi & bean salad: Energy 393kcal/1635kJ; Protein 16.5g; Carbohydrate 20.8g, of which sugars 3.4g; Fat 27.7g, of which saturates 9.4g; Cholesterol 29mg; Calcium 263mg; Fibre 6.3g; Sodium 215mg
Roasted shallots & butternut squash: Energy 275kcal/1136kJ; Protein 7.7g; Carbohydrate 9.3g, of which sugars 7g; Fat 23.2g, of which saturates 5.6g; Cholesterol 18mg; Calcium 165mg; Fibre 2.9g; Sodium 541mg

Potato & Feta Salad with a Mustard Dressing

This flavourful potato salad is easy to assemble – a perfect lunch for a busy day.

Serves 4

115g/4oz feta cheese
500g/1¼lb small new potatoes
5 spring onions (scallions), green and white parts finely chopped
15ml/1 tbsp rinsed bottled capers
8–10 black olives
45ml/3 tbsp finely chopped fresh flat leaf parsley
30ml/2 tbsp finely chopped mint
salt and ground black pepper

For the dressing

90–120ml/6–8 tbsp extra virgin olive oil
juice of 1 lemon, or to taste
45ml/3 tbsp Greek (US strained plain) yogurt
45ml/3 tbsp finely chopped fresh dill, plus a few sprigs, to garnish
5ml/1 tsp French mustard

1 Chop the feta cheese into small, even cubes and crumble slightly into a bowl. Set aside.

2 Bring a pan of lightly salted water to the boil and cook the potatoes in their skins for 25–30 minutes, or until tender. Take care not to let them become soggy and disintegrate. Drain them thoroughly and let them cool a little.

3 When the potatoes are cool enough to handle, peel them with your fingers and place them in a large bowl. If they are very small, keep them whole; otherwise cut them into large cubes. Add the chopped spring onions, capers, olives, feta cheese and fresh herbs, and toss gently to mix.

4 To make the dressing, place the extra virgin olive oil in a bowl with the lemon juice. Whisk thoroughly for a few minutes until the dressing emulsifies and thickens; you may need to add a little more olive oil if it does not thicken.

5 Whisk in the yogurt, dill and mustard, with salt and pepper to taste. Dress the salad while the potatoes are still warm, tossing lightly to coat them.

Aubergine & Butternut Salad with Crumbled Feta

This delightful salad not only tastes good, but looks very appetizing. Watch out for slivered pistachios in Middle-Eastern shops: their colour combines brilliantly with the orange butternut.

Serves 4

2 aubergines (eggplants)
1 butternut squash, about 1kg/2¼lb, peeled
120ml/4fl oz/½ cup extra virgin olive oil
5ml/1 tsp paprika
150g/5oz feta cheese
50g/2oz/⅓ cup pistachio nuts, roughly chopped
salt and ground black pepper

1 Slice the aubergines widthways into 5mm/¼in rounds. Spread them out on a tray and sprinkle with a little salt. Leave for 30 minutes. Slice the squash in the same way, scooping out any seeds with a spoon. Place the butternut squash slices in a bowl, season lightly and toss with 30ml/2 tbsp of the oil.

2 Heat the griddle until a few drops of water sprinkled onto the surface evaporate instantly. Lower the heat a little and cook the butternut squash slices in batches. Sear for about 1½ minutes on each side, then put them on a tray. Continue until all the slices have been cooked, then dust with paprika.

3 Pat the aubergine slices dry. Toss with the remaining oil and season lightly. Cook in the same way as the squash. Mix the cooked aubergine and squash together in a bowl. Crumble the feta over the warm salad, scatter the chopped pistachio nuts over the top and dust with the remaining paprika.

Cook's Tip
The vegetables are also delicious cooked directly on a charcoal barbecue. When the coals are medium-hot, sear the vegetables for about 2 minutes on each side.

Potato & feta salad: Energy 138Kcal/566kJ; Protein 1.3g; carbohydrate 1.2g, of which sugars 1.1g; Fat 14.2g, of which saturates 2g; Cholesterol 0mg; Caclium 75mg;Fibre 1.4g; Sodium 40mg
Aubergine & butternut salad: Energy 385kcal/1593kJ; Protein 10.7g; Carbohydrate 9.2g, of which sugars 7g; Fat 34.2g, of which saturates 9.1g; Cholesterol 26mg; Calcium 231mg; Fibre 4.8g; Sodium 608mg

Roquefort & Walnut Salad

This delicious, fresh-tasting salad makes a wonderful light lunch dish. The combination of luxurious fresh figs with the tangy blue cheese and crunchy nuts is quite exquisite.

Serves 4

45ml/3 tbsp walnut oil
juice of 1 lemon
mixed salad leaves
4 fresh figs
115g/4oz Roquefort cheese, cut into small chunks
75g/3oz/¾ cup walnut halves
salt and ground black pepper

1 Whisk together the walnut oil and lemon juice in a bowl until emulsified, then season with salt and pepper.

2 Wash and dry the salad leaves then tear them gently into bitesize pieces. Place in a mixing bowl and toss with the dressing. Transfer to a large serving dish or divide among four individual plates, ensuring a good balance of colour and texture on each plate.

3 Cut the figs into quarters and add to the salad leaves. Sprinkle the cheese over the salad, crumbling it slightly. Then sprinkle over the walnuts, breaking them up roughly in your fingers as you work. Serve immediately.

Cook's Tip
Look for dark green salad leaves, such as lamb's lettuce and rocket (arugula), and reds, such as lollo rosso, as well as some crunchy leaves, such as Little Gem (Bibb), to add interest.

Variation
The figs may be replaced with ripe nectarines or peaches if you prefer. Wash and cut in half, discard the stone (pit), then cut each half into three or four slices. If the skin is very tough, you may need to remove it completely.

Roquefort & Flageolet Bean Salad with Honey Dressing

Pungent and creamy, classic sheep's milk Roquefort goes particularly well with pale green flageolet beans and a light sweet-sour dressing.

Serves 4

150g/5oz/scant 1 cup dried flageolet or cannellini beans, soaked overnight in water
1 bay leaf
1 sprig of thyme
1 small onion, sliced
30ml/2 tbsp chopped parsley
30ml/2 tbsp chopped walnuts
200g/7oz Roquefort cheese, lightly crumbled
salt and ground black pepper
red and green salad leaves, to serve

For the dressing
60ml/4 tbsp extra virgin olive oil
30ml/2 tbsp rice wine vinegar or half wine vinegar and half water
5ml/1 tsp French mustard
10ml/2 tsp clear honey

1 Drain the beans and put them in a pan. Cover with cold water. Bring to the boil. Cook for 10 minutes, then reduce the heat. Add the bay leaf, thyme and onion and simmer for 20–25 minutes until the beans are tender.

2 Drain the beans, discarding the herbs but not the onion. Transfer to a bowl, season and leave until just warm.

3 To make the dressing, mix the oil, vinegar or vinegar and water, mustard and honey in a small bowl. Add salt to taste and a generous grinding of black pepper. Pour over the beans. Add the parsley and walnuts.

4 Gently mix the crumbled Roquefort into the salad. Serve the salad at room temperature with red and green salad leaves.

Variation
Try using another flavourful blue cheese instead of Roquefort. The salad is also great with cooked lentils instead of the beans.

Roquefort & walnut salad: Energy 415Kcal/1726kJ; Protein 10.6g; Carbohydrate 26.6g, of which sugars 26.4g; Fat 30.3g, of which saturates 7.3g; Cholesterol 22mg; Calcium 286mg; fibre 4.5g; sodium 383mg
Roquefort & flageolet bean salad: Energy 524kcal/2179kJ; Protein 25.3g; Carbohydrate 20.2g, of which sugars 4.2g; Fat 38.5g, of which saturates 16.4g; Cholesterol 56mg; Calcium 440mg; Fibre 7g; Sodium 927mg

Quail's Egg Salad with Bishop Kennedy Cheese

Bishop Kennedy is produced in Scotland and is a full-fat soft cheese, with its rind washed in malt whisky to produce a distinctive orangey red crust and a strong creamy taste. It is perfect combined with softly cooked quail's eggs in this unusual salad. If the cheese is unavailable, use another variety with lots of flavour.

Serves 4

8 quail's eggs
vinegar, for poaching
½ red onion, finely chopped
½ leek, cut into fine strips and blanched
75g/3oz Bishop Kennedy cheese, finely diced
½ red cabbage, shredded
mixed salad leaves, including Little Gem (Bibb) lettuce and lollo bionda
10ml/2 tsp pine nuts
French dressing, to serve

1 To poach the quail's eggs you need a shallow pan of simmering water with a dash of vinegar added, an eggcup, a slotted spoon, a pan of iced water. Using a thin knife, carefully break the shell of an egg and open it up into the eggcup.

2 Gently lower the cup into the simmering water, allowing some water to cover and firm up the egg, then let it slide into the water and cook for about 2 minutes. The white should change from opaque to just white. Lift the egg out with a slotted spoon and put it straight into iced water.

3 When all the eggs are cooked lift them out of the water and dry them on kitchen paper. This last bit can be done just before you assemble the salad since the quail's eggs will keep in cold water for up to 2 days.

4 Combine the salad ingredients, including the pine nuts (which can be lightly toasted if you like).

5 Toss with French dressing to coat. To serve, place the diced Bishop Kennedy and the quail's eggs on top of the salad.

Springtime Salad with Quail's Eggs

Enjoy some of the best early season garden vegetables in this crunchy green salad. Quail's eggs add a lovely touch of sophistication and elegance.

Serves 4

175g/6oz broad (fava) beans
175g/6oz fresh peas
175g/6oz asparagus
175g/6oz very small new potatoes, scrubbed
45ml/3 tbsp good lemon mayonnaise
45ml/3 tbsp soured cream or crème fraîche
½ bunch fresh mint, chopped, plus whole leaves for garnishing
8 quail's eggs, soft-boiled and peeled
salt and ground black pepper

1 Cook the broad beans, peas, asparagus and new potatoes in separate pans of lightly salted boiling water until just tender. Drain, refresh under cold water, and drain again.

2 When the vegetables are completely cold, mix them lightly together in a large bowl.

3 Mix the mayonnaise with the soured cream or crème fraîche and chopped mint in a bowl. Stir in salt and pepper, if needed.

4 Pour the dressing over the salad and toss to coat.

5 Add the quail's eggs and whole mint leaves and toss very gently to mix. Serve immediately.

Cook's Tip

To make your own lemon mayonnaise, combine two egg yolks, 5ml/1 tsp Dijon mustard, and the grated (shredded) rind and juice of half a lemon in a blender or food processor. Add salt and pepper to taste. Process to combine. With the motor running, add about 250ml/8fl oz/1 cup mild olive oil (or a mixture of olive oil and sunflower oil) through the lid or feeder tube, until the mixture emulsifies. Trickle the oil in at first, then add it in a steady stream.

Quail's egg salad: Energy 231kcal/956kJ; Protein 11.7g; Carbohydrate 5.3g, of which sugars 4,8g; Fat 17.7g, of which saturates 5.6g; Cholesterol 132mg; Calcium 203mg; Fibre 2.3g; Sodium 183mg
Springtime salad: Energy 256kcal/1067kJ; Protein 12.5g; Carbohydrate 19.3g, of which sugars 3.6g; Fat 14.9g, of which saturates 3.7g; Cholesterol 110mg; Calcium 100mg; Fibre 6.1g; Sodium 101mg

Chilli Salad Omelette with Hummus

These delicate omelettes filled with healthy and nutritious salad make a refreshing lunch option. The omelettes are made in advance for quick, last-minute assembly.

Serves 4

4 eggs
15ml/1 tbsp cornflour (cornstarch)
15ml/1 tbsp water
115g/4oz/1 cup shredded salad vegetables
60ml/4 tbsp chilli salad dressing
60–75ml/4–5 tbsp hummus
4 cooked bacon rashers (strips), chopped
salt and ground black pepper

1 Beat together the eggs, cornflour and the water.

2 Heat a lightly oiled frying pan and pour a quarter of the mixture into the pan, tipping it to spread it out evenly.

3 Cook the omelette gently. Carefully remove it from the pan once cooked, then make three more omelettes in the same way. Stack the omelettes between sheets of baking parchment, then chill.

4 When ready to serve, toss the shredded salad vegetables together with about 45ml/3 tbsp of the chilli salad dressing.

5 Spread half of each omelette with hummus, top with the dressed salad vegetables and chopped cooked bacon, and fold in half.

6 Drizzle the rest of the dressing over the filled omelettes before serving.

Cook's Tip
Chilli salad dressing should be available in most big supermarkets.

Fried Egg Salad

Chillies and eggs may seem unlikely partners, but they actually work well together. The peppery flavour of the watercress makes it the perfect foundation for this tasty salad.

Serves 2

15ml/1 tbsp groundnut (peanut) oil
1 garlic clove, thinly sliced
4 eggs
2 shallots, thinly sliced
2 small fresh red chillies, seeded and thinly sliced
½ small cucumber, finely diced
1cm/½in piece fresh root ginger, peeled and grated
juice of 2 limes
30ml/2 tbsp soy sauce
5ml/1 tsp caster (superfine) sugar
small bunch coriander (cilantro)
bunch watercress, coarsely chopped

1 Heat the oil in a frying pan. Add the garlic and cook over a low heat until it starts to turn golden.

2 Crack in the eggs. Break the yolks with a wooden spatula, then fry until the eggs are almost firm. Remove from the pan and set aside.

3 Mix the shallots, chillies, cucumber and ginger in a bowl. In a separate bowl, whisk the lime juice with the soy sauce and caster sugar. Pour this dressing over the vegetables and toss lightly together.

4 Reserve a few coriander sprigs for the garnish. Chop the rest and add to the salad. Toss it again.

5 Reserve a few watercress sprigs and arrange the remainder on two plates. Cut the fried eggs into slices and divide them between the watercress mounds. Spoon the shallot mixture over them and serve, garnished with coriander and watercress.

Variation
For a milder version, omit the chilli and add chopped red (bell) pepper: roast the pepper first, for a sweeter flavour.

Chilli salad omelettes: Energy 173kcal/720kJ; Protein 11.8g; Carbohydrate 5.7g, of which sugars 0.8g; Fat 11.7g, of which saturates 3.1g; Cholesterol 204mg; Calcium 45mg; Fibre 0.6g; Sodium 558mg
Fried egg salad: Energy 235kcal/977kJ; Protein 14.8g; Carbohydrate 6.4g, of which sugars 5.6g; Fat 17.2g, of which saturates 3.9g; Cholesterol 381mg; Calcium 154mg; Fibre 1.2g; Sodium 1234mg

Artichoke & Egg Salad

Artichoke hearts are best when cut from fresh artichokes, but can also be bought frozen.

Serves 4

4 large artichokes or 4 frozen artichoke hearts, thawed
½ lemon
4 eggs, hard-boiled
fresh parsley sprigs, to garnish

For the mayonnaise
1 egg yolk
10ml/2 tsp Dijon mustard
15ml/1 tbsp white wine vinegar
250ml/8 fl oz/1 cup olive or vegetable oil
30ml/2 tbsp chopped fresh parsley
salt and ground black pepper

1 If using fresh artichokes, wash them. Squeeze the lemon and put the juice and the squeezed half in a bowl of cold water.

2 Prepare the artichokes one at a time. Cut off only the tip from the stem. Peel the stem with a small knife, pulling upwards towards the leaves. Pull off the small leaves around the stem and continue snapping off the upper part of the dark outer leaves until you reach the taller inner leaves. Cut the tops off the leaves with a sharp knife. Place the artichoke in the acidulated water. Repeat with the other artichokes.

3 Boil or steam the fresh artichokes until just tender (when a leaf comes away easily when pulled). Cook frozen artichoke hearts according to the packet instructions. Allow them to cool completely.

4 To make the mayonnaise, combine the egg yolk, mustard and vinegar in a mixing bowl. Add salt and pepper to taste. Add the oil in a thin stream, beating with a wire whisk. When thick and smooth, stir in the parsley. Cover and chill until needed.

5 If using fresh artichokes, pull off the leaves. Cut the stems off level with the base. Scrape off the hairy 'choke' with a knife.

6 Shell the eggs. Cut the eggs and artichokes into wedges. Arrange on a serving plate, spoon the mayonnaise over the top, garnish with parsley sprigs and serve.

Warm Dressed Salad with Poached Eggs

Soft poached eggs, hot croûtons and cool, crisp salad leaves with a warm dressing make a lively and unusual combination.

Serves 2

½ small loaf Granary (whole-wheat) bread
45ml/3 tbsp walnut oil
2 eggs
115g/4oz mixed salad leaves
45ml/3 tbsp extra virgin olive oil
2 garlic cloves, crushed
15ml/1 tbsp balsamic or sherry vinegar
50g/2oz piece of Parmesan cheese, shaved
ground black pepper (optional)

1 Carefully cut off the crust from the Granary loaf and discard it. Cut the bread into 2.5cm/1in cubes.

2 Heat the walnut oil in a large, heavy frying pan (skillet). Add the bread cubes and cook over a low heat for about 5 minutes, turning and tossing the cubes occasionally, until they are crisp and golden brown all over.

3 Bring a pan of water to the boil. Break each egg into a cup, one at a time, and carefully slide each one into the water. Gently poach the eggs over a low heat for about 4 minutes, until lightly cooked and the whites have just set.

4 Meanwhile, divide the salad leaves among two plates. Arrange the croûtons over the leaves.

5 Wipe the frying pan clean with kitchen paper. Heat the olive oil in the pan, add the garlic and vinegar and cook over a high heat for 1 minute. Pour the warm dressing over the salad on each plate.

6 Lift out each poached egg, in turn, with a slotted spoon and place one on top of each of the salads. Top with thin shavings of Parmesan and a little freshly ground black pepper, to taste.

Artichoke & egg salad: Energy 493kcal/2034kJ; Protein 7.9g; Carbohydrate 1.3g, of which sugars 1.2g; Fat 51g, of which saturates 7.1g; Cholesterol 241mg; Calcium 100mg; Fibre 1.7g; Sodium 137mg
Warm dressed salad: Energy 908kcal/3803kJ; Protein 35.3g; Carbohydrate 94.8g, of which sugars 5.8g; Fat 45.8g, of which saturates 10.9g; Cholesterol 215mg; Calcium 747mg; Fibre 6.6g; Sodium 1433mg

Coronation Salad

The famous salad dressing used in this dish was created especially for the coronation dinner of Queen Elizabeth II. It is a wonderful accompaniment to hard-boiled eggs and vegetables.

Serves 6

450g/1lb new potatoes
45ml/3 tbsp French dressing
3 spring onions (scallions), chopped
6 eggs, hard-boiled and halved
frilly lettuce leaves
¼ cucumber, cut into thin strips
6 large radishes, sliced
1 carton salad cress
salt and ground black pepper

For the coronation dressing
30ml/2 tbsp olive oil
1 small onion, chopped
15ml/1 tbsp mild curry powder or korma spice mix
10ml/2 tsp tomato purée (paste)
30ml/2 tbsp lemon juice
30ml/2 tbsp sherry
300ml/½ pint/1¼ cups mayonnaise
150ml/¼ pint/⅔ cup natural (plain) yogurt

1 Boil the potatoes in salted water until tender. Drain, then transfer to a large bowl and toss in the French dressing while they are still warm.

2 Stir in the spring onions and the salt and pepper to taste, and allow to cool thoroughly.

3 Meanwhile, make the coronation dressing. Heat the oil in a small pan and fry the onion for 3 minutes, until soft. Stir in the curry powder or spice mix and fry for a further 1 minute. Remove from the heat and mix in the tomato purée, lemon juice, sherry, mayonnaise and yogurt.

4 Stir the dressing into the potatoes, add the eggs, then chill. Line a serving platter with lettuce leaves and pile the salad in the centre. Scatter over the cucumber, radishes and cress.

Cook's Tip
Make your own mayonnaise and French dressing, if time allows.

Avocado, Tomato & Mozzarella Pasta Salad

When avocados are in season, there is no better way to serve them than with juicy tomatoes in a simple pasta salad.

Serves 4

175g/6oz dried farfalle (pasta bows)
6 ripe red tomatoes
225g/8oz mozzarella cheese
1 large ripe avocado
30ml/2 tbsp pine nuts, toasted
1 fresh basil sprig, to garnish

For the dressing
90ml/6 tbsp olive oil
30ml/2 tbsp wine vinegar
5ml/1 tsp balsamic vinegar (optional)
5ml/1 tsp wholegrain mustard
pinch of sugar
salt and ground black pepper
chopped fresh basil, to garnish

1 Cook the pasta in plenty of boiling salted water according to the packet instructions. Drain well and cool.

2 Slice the tomatoes and mozzarella into thin rounds. Halve the avocado, remove the stone (pit), and peel off the skin. Slice the flesh lengthwise.

3 Whisk together all the dressing ingredients, except the chopped fresh basil, in a small bowl.

4 Just before you are ready to serve, arrange alternate slices of tomato, mozzarella and avocado in a spiral pattern, just slightly overlapping, around the edge of a large serving platter.

5 Toss the pasta with half the dressing and the chopped basil. Pile into the centre of the platter. Pour over the remaining dressing, scatter over the pine nuts and garnish with basil.

Cook's Tip
To ripen avocados, put them into a paper bag with an apple or potato and leave in a warm place for 2–3 days.

Coronation salad: Energy 587kcal/2429kJ; Protein 10.1g; Carbohydrate 17.1g, of which sugars 4.7g; Fat 51.6g, of which saturates 8.8g; Cholesterol 228mg; Calcium 97mg; Fibre 1.1g; Sodium 401mg
Avocado, tomato & mozzarella: Energy 585kcal/2436kJ; Protein 18.3g; Carbohydrate 36.9g, of which sugars 5.4g; Fat 41.4g, of which saturates 12.2g; Cholesterol 33mg; Calcium 228mg; Fibre 3.8g; Sodium 236mg

Roquefort & Walnut Pasta Salad

This is a simple, earthy salad, relying totally on the quality of the ingredients. Crisp salad leaves, crunchy walnuts and tender pasta provide a sumptuous combination of tastes and textures.

Serves 4

225g/8oz/2 cups dried pasta shapes, such as penne
selection of salad leaves, such as rocket (arugula), frisée, lamb's lettuce, spinach or radicchio
30ml/2 tbsp walnut oil
60ml/4 tbsp sunflower oil
30ml/2 tbsp red wine vinegar or sherry vinegar
225g/8oz Roquefort cheese, roughly crumbled
115g/4oz/1 cup walnut halves
salt and ground black pepper

1 Bring a large pan of salted water to the boil, add the pasta and cook according to the packet instructions, until al dente. Drain well and cool.

2 Place the salad leaves in a bowl.

3 Whisk together the walnut oil, sunflower oil and vinegar. Season with salt and ground black pepper to taste.

4 Pile the cooked, cooled pasta in the centre of the salad leaves and scatter over the crumbled Roquefort.

5 Pour over the dressing and sprinkle the walnuts over the top. Toss the salad just before serving.

Cook's Tips

- *Toast the walnuts under the grill (broiler) to add extra flavour.*
- *Look for dark green salad leaves, such as lamb's lettuce and rocket (arugula), and reds, such as lollo rosso, as well as some crunchy leaves, such as Little Gem (Bibb), to give an interesting and nutritious variety.*

Couscous with Eggs & Tomato

This tasty Middle-Eastern vegetarian dish is quick to make with the easy-to-use couscous available today.

Serves 4

675g/1½lb plum tomatoes, roughly chopped
4 garlic cloves, chopped
75ml/5 tbsp olive oil
½ fresh red chilli, seeded and chopped
10ml/2 tsp soft light brown sugar
4 eggs
1 large onion, chopped
2 celery sticks, finely sliced
50g/2oz/⅓ cup sultanas (golden raisins)
200g/7oz/generous 1 cup ready-to-use couscous
350ml/12fl oz/1½ cups hot vegetable stock
salt and ground black pepper

1 Preheat the oven to 200°C/400°F/Gas 6. Spread out the tomatoes and garlic in a roasting pan, drizzle with 30ml/2 tbsp of the oil, sprinkle with the chopped chilli and sugar, salt and pepper, and roast for 20 minutes.

2 Meanwhile, cook the eggs in boiling water for 4 minutes, then plunge them straight into cold water and leave until cold. Carefully peel off the shells.

3 Heat 15–30ml/1–2 tbsp of the remaining olive oil in a large pan and fry the onion and celery until softened. Add the sultanas, couscous and hot stock, and set aside until all the liquid has been absorbed. Stir gently, adding extra hot stock if necessary, and season to taste. Turn the mixture into a large heated serving dish, bury the eggs in the couscous and cover with foil. Keep warm in the oven.

4 Remove the tomato mixture from the oven and press it through a strainer placed over a bowl. Add 15ml/1 tbsp boiling water and the rest of the olive oil and stir to make a smooth, rich sauce.

5 Remove the couscous mixture from the oven and locate the eggs. Spoon a little tomato sauce over the top of each egg. Serve immediately, with the rest of the sauce handed separately.

Roquefort & walnut pasta salad: Energy 731kcal/3042kJ; Protein 22.5g; Carbohydrate 42.6g, of which sugars 2.6g; Fat 53.5g, of which saturates 14.3g; Cholesterol 42mg; Calcium 316mg; Fibre 2.7g; Sodium 690mg
Couscous with eggs & tomato: Energy 418kcal/1744kJ; Protein 12.1g; Carbohydrate 49.3g, of which sugars 21g; Fat 20.6g, of which saturates 3.7g; Cholesterol 190mg; Calcium 85mg; Fibre 3.4g; Sodium 99mg

White Beans with Green Peppers in Spicy Dressing

Tender white beans are delicious in this spicy sauce with the bite of fresh, crunchy green pepper.

Serves 4

750g/1⅔lb tomatoes, diced
1 onion, finely chopped
½–1 mild fresh chilli, finely chopped
1 green (bell) pepper, seeded and chopped
pinch of sugar
4 garlic cloves, chopped
400g/14oz can cannellini beans, drained
45–60ml/3–4 tbsp olive oil
grated rind and juice of 1 lemon
15ml/1 tbsp cider vinegar or wine vinegar
salt and ground black pepper
chopped fresh parsley, to garnish

1 Put the diced tomatoes, chopped onion, chilli and green pepper, sugar, chopped garlic, cannellini beans, salt and plenty of ground black pepper in a large bowl and toss together until well combined.

2 Add the olive oil, grated lemon rind, lemon juice and cider vinegar or wine vinegar to the salad and toss lightly to combine all of the ingredients in the dressing.

3 Chill before serving, garnished with chopped parsley.

Cook's Tip
When chopping chillies it is important to take care and wash your hands afterwards, as they can irritate the skin and eyes. You could wear gloves.

Variation
Substitute flageolets (small cannellini) for the cannellini beans, or try using haricot (navy) beans. They all taste and look attractive.

White Bean Salad with Roasted Red Pepper Dressing

The speckled herb and red pepper dressing adds a wonderful colour contrast to this salad, which is best served warm. Canned beans are used for convenience – substitute cooked, dried beans, if you prefer.

Serves 4

1 large red (bell) pepper
60ml/4 tbsp olive oil
1 large garlic clove, crushed
25g/1oz/1 cup fresh oregano leaves or flat leaf parsley
15ml/1 tbsp balsamic vinegar
400g/14oz/3 cups canned flageolet (small cannellini) beans, drained and rinsed
200g/7oz/1 1/2 cups can cannellini beans, drained and rinsed
salt and ground black pepper

1 Preheat the oven to 200°C/400°F/Gas 6. Place the red pepper on a baking sheet, brush with oil and roast for 30 minutes or until the skin blisters and the flesh is soft.

2 Remove the pepper from the oven and place in a plastic bag. Seal and leave to cool. (This makes the skin easier to remove.)

3 When the pepper is cool enough to handle, remove it from the bag and peel off the skin. Rinse under cold running water. Slice the pepper in half, remove the seeds and dice. Set aside.

4 Heat the remaining oil in a pan and cook the garlic for 1 minute until soft. Remove from the heat, then add the oregano, the red pepper and any juices, and the balsamic vinegar.

5 Put the beans in a large bowl and pour over the dressing. Season to taste, then stir gently. Serve warm.

Cook's Tip
Low in fat, cannellini beans should be a regular part of a healthy balanced diet. They are also a good source of minerals.

White beans with green peppers: Energy 226kcal/947kJ; Protein 8.8g; Carbohydrate 27.6g, of which sugars 12.9g; Fat 9.6g, of which saturates 1.5g; Cholesterol 0mg; Calcium 92mg; Fibre 9g; Sodium 409mg
White bean salad: Energy 165kcal/686kJ; Protein 4.1g; Carbohydrate 11.9g, of which sugars 4.6g; Fat 11.6g, of which saturates 1.7g; Cholesterol 0mg; Calcium 52mg; Fibre 4.1g; Sodium 199mg

Warm Black-eyed Bean Salad with Rocket

This is an easy dish, as black-eyed beans do not need to be soaked overnight. By adding spring onions and lots of aromatic dill, they are transformed into a refreshing and healthy meal.

Serves 4

275g/10oz/1½ cups black-eyed beans (peas)
5 spring onions (scallions), sliced into rounds
a large handful of fresh rocket (arugula) leaves, chopped if large
45–60ml/3–4 tbsp chopped fresh dill
150ml/¼ pint/⅔ cup extra virgin olive oil
juice of 1 lemon, or to taste
10–12 black olives
salt and ground black pepper
small cos or romaine lettuce leaves, to serve

1 Thoroughly rinse the beans and drain them well. Turn them into a pan and pour in cold water to just about cover them. Slowly bring to the boil over a low heat. As soon as the water is boiling, remove the pan from the heat and drain the water off immediately.

2 Put the beans back in the pan with fresh cold water to cover and add a pinch of salt – this will make their skins harder and stop them from disintegrating when they are cooked.

3 Bring the beans to the boil over a medium heat, then lower the heat and cook them until they are soft but not mushy. They will take 20–30 minutes only, so keep an eye on them.

4 Drain the beans, reserving 75–90ml/5–6 tbsp of the cooking liquid. Transfer the beans to a large salad bowl. Immediately add the spring onions, rocket, dill, oil, lemon juice, olives and the reserved liquid. Season with salt and pepper, then mix well.

5 Serve immediately, piled onto the lettuce leaves, or leave to cool slightly and serve later.

Bean Feast with Tomato & Avocado Salsa

This is a very quick and easy recipe using canned beans, although it could be made with dried beans, if you like.

Serves 4

15ml/1 tbsp olive oil
1 small onion, finely chopped
3 garlic cloves, finely chopped
1 fresh red Ancho chilli, seeded and finely chopped
1 red (bell) pepper, seeded and coarsely chopped
2 plum tomatoes, chopped
2 bay leaves
10ml/2 tsp chopped fresh oregano
10ml/2 tsp ground cumin
5ml/1 tsp ground coriander
2.5ml/½ tsp ground cloves
15ml/1 tbsp soft dark brown sugar
400g/14oz can red kidney beans, rinsed and drained
400g/14oz can flageolet (small cannellini) or cannellini beans, rinsed, drained
400g/14oz can borlotti beans, rinsed and drained
300ml/½ pint/1¼ cups vegetable stock
salt and ground black pepper
fresh coriander (cilantro), to garnish

For the salsa

1 ripe, but firm, avocado
45ml/3 tbsp fresh lime juice
1 small red onion, chopped
1 small fresh hot green chilli, seeded and chopped
5 ripe plum tomatoes, skinned and chopped
45ml/3 tbsp chopped fresh coriander (cilantro)

1 Heat the oil and fry the onion for 3 minutes, until softened. Add the garlic, chilli, pepper, tomatoes, herbs and spices.

2 Stir well and cook for a further 3 minutes, then add the sugar, beans and stock and cook for 8 minutes. Season with salt and plenty of ground black pepper.

3 To make the salsa, peel and stone (pit) the avocado. Cut the flesh into 1cm/½in dice. Place in a bowl with the lime juice and stir to mix. Add the red onion, chilli, tomatoes and coriander. Season with black pepper and mix. Spoon the beans into a warmed serving dish and serve with the tomato and avocado salsa, garnished with sprigs of fresh coriander.

Black-eyed bean salad: Energy 238kcal/1007kJ; Protein 16.1g; Carbohydrate 31g, of which sugars 2.4g; Fat 6.4g, of which saturates 0.9g; Cholesterol 0mg; Calcium 114mg; Fibre 12.3g; Sodium 580mg
Bean feast: Energy 463kcal/1955kJ; Protein 24.1g; Carbohydrate 72.3g, of which sugars 28.3g; Fat 10.5g, of which saturates 2g; Cholesterol 0mg; Calcium 268mg; Fibre 23.8g; Sodium 1196mg

Marinated Courgette & Flageolet Bean Salad

Serve this healthy salad as a light meal or as an accompaniment to a main course. It has a wonderful bright green colour and is perfect for a summer lunch.

Serves 4

2 courgettes (zucchini), halved lengthwise and sliced
400g/14oz can flageolet (small cannellini) or cannellini beans, drained and rinsed
45ml/3 tbsp garlic-infused olive oil
grated rind and juice of 1 unwaxed lemon
salt and ground black pepper

1 Cook the courgette slices in boiling salted water for 2–3 minutes, or until just tender. Drain and refresh under cold running water.

2 Transfer the drained courgettes to a bowl with the beans.

3 Stir in the oil, lemon rind and juice and some salt and ground black pepper.

4 Chill for 30 minutes before serving.

Variation
To add extra flavour to the salad add 30ml/2 tbsp chopped basil and mint before chilling.

Cook's Tip
Flageolet beans are expensive to buy and are best eaten simply in salads like this one. For an even simpler way to enjoy them, cook them until tender, then season them and drizzle over a little olive oil and lemon juice.

Bountiful Bean & Nut Salad

This is a good multi-purpose dish. It can be a cold main course, a buffet party dish, or a salad on the side.

Serves 6

75g/3oz/½ cup red kidney, pinto or borlotti beans
75g/3oz/½ cup white cannellini or butter beans
30ml/2 tbsp olive oil
175g/6oz cooked fresh green beans
3 spring onions (scallions), sliced
1 small yellow or red (bell) pepper, sliced
1 carrot, coarsely grated
30ml/2 tbsp dried topping onions or sun-dried tomatoes, chopped
50g/2oz/½ cup unsalted cashew nuts or almonds, chopped

For the dressing

45ml/3 tbsp sunflower oil
30ml/2 tbsp red wine vinegar
15ml/1 tbsp wholegrain mustard
5ml/1 tsp caster (superfine) sugar
5ml/1 tsp dried mixed herbs
salt and ground black pepper

1 Soak the beans, overnight if possible, then drain and rinse well. Place in a pan, cover with cold water and cook according to the instructions on the packet.

2 Drain the beans and transfer to a large serving bowl. Add the olive oil and season with salt and pepper. Toss well to coat, then leave to cool for 30 minutes.

3 Add the green beans, spring onions, peppers and carrot to the bowl and stir to combine.

4 To make the dressing, put all the ingredients in a jar, close the lid tightly and shake to mix. Toss the dressing into the salad and adjust the seasoning. Serve sprinkled with the topping onions and sun-dried tomatoes, if using, and the chopped nuts.

Cook's Tip
This salad keeps well for up to 3 days in the refrigerator, making it ideal for entertaining.

Courgette & flageolet bean salad: Energy 188kcal/785kJ; Protein 8.3g; Carbohydrate 19.2g, of which sugars 4.9g; Fat 9.2g, of which saturates 1.4g; Cholesterol 0mg; Calcium 90mg; Fibre 6.9g; Sodium 391mg
Bountiful bean & nut salad: Energy 230kcal/959kJ; Protein 8.6g; Carbohydrate 17.8g, of which sugars 5.7g; Fat 14.3g, of which saturates 2.2g; Cholesterol 0mg; Calcium 51mg; Fibre 5.8g; Sodium 73mg

Green Bean Salad

You could make this lovely dish any time of the year with frozen vegetables and still get a pretty salad.

Serves 4

175g/6oz shelled broad (fava) beans
115g/4oz green beans, quartered
115g/4oz mangetouts (snow peas)
8–10 small fresh mint leaves
3 spring onions (scallions), chopped

For the dressing

60ml/4 tbsp olive oil
15ml/1 tbsp cider vinegar
15ml/1 tbsp chopped fresh mint
1 garlic clove, crushed
salt and ground black pepper

1 Plunge the broad beans into a pan of boiling water and bring back to the boil. Remove from the heat immediately and plunge into cold water. Drain.

2 Repeat the blanching process in step 1 with the green beans.

3 In a large bowl, mix the blanched broad beans and green beans with the raw mangetouts, fresh mint leaves and chopped spring onions.

4 To make the dressing, in another bowl, mix together the olive oil, cider vinegar, chopped fresh mint, crushed garlic and salt and ground black pepper.

5 Pour the dressing over the salad and toss well. Chill until ready to serve.

Cook's Tips

- *Beans and peas are a good source of protein and fibre. They are rich in vitamin C, iron, thiamine, folate, phosphorous and potassium.*
- *Look for bright-green, smooth, plump pods and keep in the refrigerator for no more than a day or two.*
- *You can also buy the beans frozen.*

Green Bean & Sweet Red Pepper Salad

A galaxy of colour and texture, with a jolt of heat from the chilli, will make this a favourite salad.

Serves 4

350g/12oz cooked green beans, quartered
2 red (bell) peppers, seeded and chopped
2 spring onions (scallions), both white and green parts, chopped
1 or more drained pickled serrano chillies, well rinsed, seeded and chopped
1 iceberg lettuce, coarsely shredded, or mixed salad leaves
green olives, to garnish

For the dressing

45ml/3 tbsp red wine vinegar
135ml/9 tbsp olive oil
salt and ground black pepper

1 Combine the green beans, peppers, spring onions and chilli(es) in a salad bowl.

2 To make the dressing, pour the vinegar into a bowl. Add salt and pepper to taste, then gradually whisk in the olive oil until well combined.

3 Pour the dressing over the prepared vegetables and toss lightly together to mix and coat thoroughly.

4 Line a large serving platter with the shredded lettuce or mixed salad leaves and arrange the vegetable mixture attractively on top. Garnish with the olives and serve.

Cook's Tip

Use a seeded, finely chopped fresh red chilli, if you prefer.

Variation

For extra flavour, top with shavings of Parmesan cheese.

Green bean salad: Energy 153kcal/637kJ; Protein 5.3g; Carbohydrate 7.6g, of which sugars 2.6g; Fat 11.5g, of which saturates 1.7g; Cholesterol 0mg; Calcium 53mg; Fibre 4.3g; Sodium 5mg
Green bean & red pepper salad: Energy 283kcal/1168kJ; Protein 3.6g; Carbohydrate 9.9g, of which sugars 8.8g; Fat 25.8g, of which saturates 3.8g; Cholesterol 0mg; Calcium 58mg; Fibre 4.1g; Sodium 7mg

Lentil, Tomato & Cheese Salad

In this hearty salad, lentils are teamed up with crumbly cheese, red onion and fresh-tasting tomatoes to provide a wholesome vegetarian main course with lots of texture contrasts. Serve with a tossed green salad and poppy seed rolls for a complete meal.

Serves 6

200g/7oz/scant 1 cup lentils (preferably Puy lentils), soaked for about 3 hours in cold water to cover
1 red onion, chopped
1 bay leaf
60ml/4 tbsp extra virgin olive oil
45ml/3 tbsp chopped fresh parsley
30ml/2 tbsp chopped fresh oregano or marjoram
250g/9oz cherry tomatoes, halved
250g/9oz feta, goat's milk cheese or Caerphilly cheese, crumbled
salt and ground black pepper
30–45ml/2–3 tbsp lightly toasted pine nuts
leaves of chicory (Belgian endive), frisée and fresh herbs, to garnish

1 Drain the lentils and place them in a large pan. Pour in plenty of cold water and add the onion and bay leaf. Bring to the boil, boil hard for 10 minutes, then lower the heat and simmer for 20 minutes or according to the instructions on the packet.

2 Drain the lentils, discard the bay leaf and transfer them to a bowl. Add salt and pepper to taste. Toss with the olive oil. Set aside to cool, then mix with the fresh parsley, oregano or marjoram and cherry tomatoes.

3 Add the cheese. Line a serving dish with chicory or frisée leaves and pile the salad in the centre. Scatter over the pine nuts and garnish with fresh herbs.

Cook's Tip
The small blue-green Puy lentils from France are perfect for salads; flat green Continental lentils or massor dhal lentils from India are also a good choice.

Fragrant Lentil & Spinach Salad

This earthy salad is great for a picnic or barbecue.

Serves 6

225g/8oz/1 cup Puy lentils
1 fresh bay leaf
1 celery stick
1 fresh thyme sprig
30ml/2 tbsp olive oil
1 onion, finely sliced
10ml/2 tsp crushed toasted cumin seeds
400g/14oz young spinach leaves
30–45ml/2–3 tbsp chopped fresh parsley, plus a few extra sprigs for garnishing
salt and ground black pepper

For the dressing

45ml/3 tbsp extra virgin olive oil
5ml/1 tsp Dijon mustard
15–25ml/3–5 tsp red wine vinegar
1 small garlic clove, finely chopped
2.5ml/½ tsp grated lemon rind

1 Rinse the lentils and place them in a large pan. Add water to cover. Tie the bay leaf, celery and thyme into a bundle and add to the pan, then bring to the boil. Lower the heat to a steady boil. Cook the lentils for 30–45 minutes, until just tender.

2 Meanwhile, make the dressing. Mix the oil and mustard with 15ml/1 tbsp of the vinegar. Add the garlic and lemon rind, and whisk to mix. Season well with salt and pepper.

3 Drain the lentils and discard the herbs. Transfer them to a serving bowl, add most of the dressing and toss well. Set aside and stir occasionally.

4 Heat the oil in a pan and cook the onion for 4–5 minutes, until it starts to soften. Add the cumin and cook for 1 minute.

5 Add the spinach and season to taste, then cover and cook for 2 minutes. Stir, then cook again briefly until wilted.

6 Stir the spinach into the lentils and leave the salad to cool to room temperature. Stir in the remaining dressing and chopped parsley. Adjust the seasoning, adding more vinegar if necessary. Spoon onto a serving platter, scatter some parsley sprigs over, and serve at room temperature with toasted French bread.

Lentil, tomato & cheese salad: Energy 341kcal/1423kJ; Protein 16.1g; Carbohydrate 22g, of which sugars 3.7g; Fat 21.6g, of which saturates 7.2g; Cholesterol 29mg; Calcium 188mg; Fibre 2.7g; Sodium 619mg
Fragrant lentil & spinach salad: Energy 224kcal/938kJ; Protein 11g; Carbohydrate 23.2g, of which sugars 2.5g; Fat 10.3g, of which saturates 1.5g; Cholesterol 0mg; Calcium 136mg; Fibre 3.4g; Sodium 132mg

Basmati & Blue Lentil Salad

Puy lentils from France (sometimes known as blue lentils) are small, deliciously nutty pulses. In this recipe, they blend beautifully with aromatic basmati rice.

Serves 6

115g/4oz/⅔cup Puys de dome lentils, soaked
225g/8oz/1¼ cups basmati rice, rinsed well
2 carrots, coarsely grated
⅓ cucumber, halved, seeded and coarsely grated
3 spring onions (scallions), sliced
45 ml/3 tbsp fresh parsley, chopped

For the dressing

30ml/2 tbsp sunflower oil
30ml/2 tbsp extra virgin olive oil
30ml/2 tbsp wine vinegar
30ml/2 tbsp fresh lemon juice
good pinch of sugar
salt and ground black pepper

1 Soak the dried lentils in plenty of cold water for 30 minutes.

2 To make the dressing, put the sunflower oil, olive oil, wine vinegar and lemon juice in a screw-topped jar. Shake until combined, then add sugar and salt and ground black pepper to taste. Set aside.

3 Drain the lentils, then pour them into a large pan of unsalted water. Bring this to the boil and cook the lentils for 20–25 minutes or until soft. Drain thoroughly.

4 Boil the basmati rice for 10 minutes, or according to the instructions on the packet, then drain.

5 Using a large mixing bowl, toss together the cooked rice and lentils in the dressing and season well. Leave, uncovered, to cool.

6 Once the rice mixture is cold, add the prepared carrots, cucumber, onions and parsley. Put the salad in the refrigerator to chill.

7 Spoon the cooled salad into an attractive bowl when ready to serve.

Thai Rice & Sprouting Beans

Thai rice has a delicate fragrance and texture that is delicious whether served hot or cold. This salad is a colourful collection of popular Thai flavours.

Serves 6

30ml/2 tbsp sesame oil
30ml/2 tbsp fresh lime juice
1 small fresh red chilli, seeded and chopped
1 garlic clove, crushed
10ml/2 tsp grated fresh root ginger
30ml/2 tbsp light soy sauce
5ml/1 tsp clear honey
45ml/3 tbsp pineapple juice
15ml/1 tbsp wine vinegar
225g/8oz/1¼ cups Thai fragrant rice, lightly boiled
2 spring onions (scallions), sliced
2 rings canned pineapple in natural juice, chopped
150g/5oz/1¼ cups sprouted lentils or beansprouts
1 small red (bell) pepper, sliced
1 celery stick, sliced
50g/2oz/½ cup unsalted cashew nuts, roughly chopped
30ml/2 tbsp toasted sesame seeds
salt and ground black pepper

1 Whisk together the sesame oil, fresh lime juice, chopped chilli, crushed garlic, grated ginger, soy sauce, honey, pineapple juice and wine vinegar in a large bowl.

2 Stir in the lightly boiled Thai fragrant rice.

3 Toss in all the remaining ingredients and mix well.

4 This dish can be served either warm or lightly chilled. If the rice grains stick together on cooling, simply stir them with a metal spoon.

Cook's Tip

Beansprouts are quite remarkable in terms of nutritional content. Once the seed (or pulse or grain) has germinated, the nutritional value rises dramatically. There are almost 30 per cent more B vitamins and 60 per cent more vitamin C in the sprout than the original seed, pulse or grain.

Basmati & blue lentil salad: Energy 231kcal/961kJ; Protein 4.2g; Carbohydrate 34.3g, of which sugars 2.2g; Fat 8.4g, of which saturates 1.2g; Cholesterol 1mg; Calcium 39mg; Fibre 1.2g; Sodium 16mg
Thai rice & sprouting beans: Energy 281kcal/1171kJ; Protein 6.7g; Carbohydrate 38.2g, of which sugars 6.6g; Fat 11.3g, of which saturates 1.8g; Cholesterol 0mg; Calcium 60mg; Fibre 1.8g; Sodium 387mg

Fruity Brown Rice Salad

An Oriental-style dressing gives this colourful rice salad extra piquancy.

Serves 4–6

115g/4oz/⅔ cup brown rice
1 small red (bell) pepper, seeded and diced
200g/7oz can corn kernels, drained
45ml/3 tbsp sultanas (golden raisins)
225g/8oz can pineapple pieces in fruit juice
15ml/1 tbsp light soy sauce
15ml/1 tbsp sunflower oil
15ml/1 tbsp hazelnut oil
1 garlic clove, crushed
5ml/1 tsp finely chopped fresh root ginger
salt and ground black pepper
4 spring onions (scallions), diagonally sliced, to garnish

1 Bring a large pan of salted water to the boil and cook the brown rice for about 30 minutes, or until it is just tender. Drain thoroughly and rinse under cold water. Drain again and leave to cool.

2 Turn the rice into a bowl and add the red pepper, corn and sultanas. Drain the pineapple pieces, reserving the juice, then add them to the rice mixture and toss lightly.

3 Pour the reserved pineapple juice into a clean screw-top jar. Add the soy sauce, sunflower and hazelnut oils, garlic and chopped root ginger and season to taste with salt and pepper. Close the jar tightly and shake vigorously.

4 Pour the dressing over the salad and toss well. Scatter the spring onions over the top and serve.

Cook's Tips

- *Hazelnut oil gives a distinctive flavour to any salad dressing and is especially good for leafy salads that need a bit of a lift. It is like olive oil, in that it contains mainly monounsaturated fats.*
- *Brown rice is often mistakenly called wholegrain. In fact, the outer husk is completely inedible and is removed from all rice, but the bran layer is left intact on brown rice.*

Wilted Spinach with Rice & Dill

This is a delicious vegetarian dish that can be made in very little time. In Greece it is particularly popular during periods of fasting, when meat is avoided for religious reasons.

Serves 6

675g/1½lb fresh spinach, trimmed of any hard stalks
105ml/7 tbsp extra virgin olive oil
1 large onion, chopped
juice of ½ lemon
150ml/¼ pint/⅔ cup water
115g/4oz/generous ½ cup long grain rice
30ml/2 tbsp chopped fresh dill, plus extra sprigs to garnish
salt and ground black pepper

1 Thoroughly wash the spinach in cold water and drain. Repeat four or five times until the spinach is completely clean and free of grit, then drain thoroughly. Brush off the excess water with kitchen paper and coarsely shred the spinach.

2 Heat the olive oil in a large pan and sauté the onion until softened. Add the spinach and stir for a few minutes to coat it with the oil.

3 As soon as the spinach looks wilted, add the lemon juice and the measured water and bring to the boil. Add the rice and chopped dill, then cover and cook gently for about 10 minutes or until the rice is cooked to your taste. If it looks too dry, add a little extra hot water.

4 Spoon the rice into a serving dish and sprinkle the sprigs of dill over the top. Serve hot or at room temperature.

Cook's Tip

This dish makes a nourishing vegetarian meal when accompanied by chickpea rissoles, served with a fresh tomato sauce. Alternatively, it is excellent as a light lunch dish, served with warm walnut bread.

Fruity brown rice salad: Energy 189kcal/799kJ; Protein 3g; Carbohydrate 35.5g, of which sugars 14.4g; Fat 4.9g, of which saturates 0.6g; Cholesterol 0mg; Calcium 20mg; Fibre 2g; Sodium 94mg
Wilted spinach with rice & dill: Energy 325kcal/1343kJ; Protein 7.8g; Carbohydrate 29.9g, of which sugars 5.6g; Fat 19.2g, of which saturates 2.7g; Cholesterol 0mg; Calcium 327mg; Fibre 4.8g; Sodium 242mg

Rice & Beans with Avocado Salsa

Tasty rice and beans, served on tortillas, with a tangy avocado and onion salsa, is a supper dish with bags of Mexican flavour.

Serves 4

40g/1½oz/¼ cup dried kidney beans or 75g/3oz/½ cup canned kidney beans, rinsed and drained
8 tomatoes, halved and seeded
2 garlic cloves, chopped
1 onion, sliced
45ml/3 tbsp olive oil
225g/8oz/generous 1 cup long grain brown rice, rinsed
600ml/1 pint/2½ cups vegetable stock
2 carrots, diced
75g/3oz/¾ cup green beans
salt and ground black pepper
4 wheat tortillas and soured cream, to serve

For the avocado salsa

1 avocado
juice of 1 lime
1 small red onion, diced
1 small fresh red chilli, seeded and chopped
15ml/1 tbsp chopped fresh coriander (cilantro)

1 If using dried kidney beans, place in a bowl, cover with cold water and leave to soak overnight, then drain and rinse well. Place in a pan with enough water to cover and bring to the boil. Boil rapidly for 10 minutes, then reduce the heat. Simmer for 40–50 minutes until tender; drain and set aside.

2 To make the avocado salsa, halve and stone (pit) the avocado. Peel and dice the flesh, then toss it in the lime juice. Add the onion, chilli and coriander. Mix well.

3 Preheat the grill (broiler) to high. Place the tomatoes, garlic and onion on a baking tray. Pour over 15ml/1 tbsp of the oil and toss to coat.

4 Grill (broil) the tomatoes, garlic and onion for 10 minutes or until the tomatoes and onions are softened, turning once. Set the vegetables aside and leave to cool.

5 Heat the remaining oil in a pan, add the rice and cook for 2 minutes, stirring, until light golden.

6 Purée the cooled tomatoes and onion in a food processor or blender, then add the mixture to the rice and cook for a further 2 minutes, stirring frequently.

7 Pour in the vegetable stock, then cover the pan and cook gently for 20 minutes, stirring occasionally.

8 Stir 30ml/2 tbsp of the kidney beans into the salsa. Add the rest to the rice mixture with the carrots and green beans, and cook for 10 minutes until the vegetables are tender.

9 Season well. Remove the pan from the heat and leave to stand, covered, for 15 minutes.

10 Meanwhile, warm the wheat tortillas under the grill. Place one tortilla on each serving plate. Spoon the hot rice and bean mixture on top. Serve immediately, with the avocado salsa and a bowl of soured cream.

Simple Rice Salad

A quick and easy dish of fresh salad vegetables tossed into cooled rice in a delicious summery dressing. Perfect for barbecues, picnics and light lunches.

Serves 6

275g/10oz/1½ cups long grain rice
1 bunch spring onions (scallions), finely sliced
1 green (bell) pepper, seeded and finely diced
1 yellow (bell) pepper, seeded and finely diced
½ fresh green chilli, chopped
225g/8oz tomatoes, peeled, seeded and chopped
30ml/2 tbsp chopped fresh flat leaf parsley or coriander

For the dressing

75ml/5 tbsp mixed olive oil and extra virgin olive oil
15ml/1 tbsp lemon juice
5ml/1 tsp strong Dijon mustard
salt and ground black pepper

1 Cook the rice in a large pan of lightly salted boiling water for 10–12 minutes, until tender.

2 Drain the rice well, rinse thoroughly under cold running water and drain again. Leave the rice to cool completely.

3 When cool, transfer the rice into a large serving bowl. Add the sliced spring onions, peppers, chilli, tomatoes and parsley or coriander.

4 To make the dressing, place all the ingredients in a screw-top jar, close the lid tightly and shake vigorously until well mixed.

5 Stir the dressing into the rice and season with salt and ground black pepper.

Cook's Tip

Similar in appearance to flat leaf parsley, fresh coriander (cilantro) has a distinctive, pungent, almost spicy flavour that makes a delicious addition to salads. If you do not like the strong flavour, use flat leaf parsley instead.

Rice & beans: Energy 390kcal/1642kJ; Protein 8g; Carbohydrate 58.4g, of which sugars 9g; Fat 15.4g, of which saturates 2.8g; Cholesterol 0mg; Calcium 49mg; Fibre 5.8g; Sodium 24mg
Simple rice salad: Energy 288kcal/1198kJ; Protein 5g; Carbohydrate 44g, of which sugars 7.1g; Fat 10.1g, of which saturates 1.5g; Cholesterol 0mg; Calcium 26mg; Fibre 2g; Sodium 57mg

Spanish Rice Salad

Ribbons of green and yellow pepper add colour and flavour to this simple salad.

Serves 6

275g/10oz/1½ cups long grain rice
1 bunch spring onions (scallions), thinly sliced
1 green (bell) pepper, seeded and sliced
1 yellow (bell) pepper, seeded and sliced
3 tomatoes, peeled, seeded and chopped
30ml/2 tbsp chopped fresh coriander (cilantro)

For the dressing
75ml/5 tbsp mixed sunflower and olive oil
15ml/1 tbsp rice vinegar
5ml/1 tsp Dijon mustard
salt and ground black pepper

1 Bring a large pan of lightly salted water to the boil and cook the rice for 10–12 minutes, until tender but still slightly firm at the centre of the grain. Do not overcook. Drain, rinse under cold water and drain again. Leave until cold.

2 Place the rice in a large serving bowl. Add the spring onions, peppers, tomatoes and coriander.

3 To make the dressing, mix the oils, vinegar and mustard in a screw-top jar with a tight-fitting lid and season to taste with salt and pepper. Shake vigorously. Stir 60–75ml/4–5 tbsp of the dressing into the rice and adjust the seasoning, if necessary.

4 Cover and chill for about 1 hour before serving. Offer the remaining dressing separately.

Variations
- *Cooked garden peas, cooked diced carrot and drained, canned sweetcorn can be added to this versatile salad.*
- *This recipe works well with long grain rice, but if you can obtain Spanish rice, it will be more authentic. This has a rounder grain, a little like risotto rice.*

Tabbouleh with Tomatoes & Apricots

A marvellous combination of vegetables and fruity flavours, this colourful dish is the epitome of Middle-Eastern cooking.

Serves 4

250g/9oz/1½ cups bulgur wheat
4 tomatoes
4 baby courgettes (zucchini), thinly sliced
4 spring onions (scallions), sliced
8 ready-to-eat dried apricots, chopped
40g/1½oz/¼ cup raisins or sultanas (golden raisins)
juice of 1 lemon
30ml/2 tbsp tomato juice
45ml/3 tbsp chopped fresh mint
1 garlic clove, crushed
salt and ground black pepper
sprig of fresh mint, to garnish

1 Put the bulgur wheat into a large bowl. Add enough cold water to come 2.5cm/1in above the level of the wheat. Leave to soak for 30 minutes, then turn into a sieve (strainer) lined with a clean dish towel. Drain well and squeeze out any water.

2 Meanwhile, cut a mark in the top of the tomatoes and plunge into boiling water for 30 seconds, then refresh in a bowl of cold water. Peel off the skins. Halve the tomatoes, remove the seeds and cores, and chop roughly.

3 In a bowl, mix the tomatoes, courgettes, spring onions and dried fruit with the bulgur wheat.

4 Put the lemon and tomato juice, mint, garlic clove and salt and pepper to taste in a small bowl and whisk together with a fork.

5 Pour the dressing over the salad and mix well. Chill for at least 1 hour. Serve garnished with a sprig of mint.

Cook's Tip
Also known as cracked wheat, bulgur wheat has been partially cooked, so it requires only a short soaking before being used in a salad. It is very handy for a quick meal.

Spanish rice salad: Energy 246kcal/1028kJ; Protein 4.7g; Carbohydrate 42.4g, of which sugars 5.6g; Fat 6.3g, of which saturates 0.8g; Cholesterol 0mg; Calcium 24mg; Fibre 1.7g; Sodium 33mg
Tabbouleh with tomatoes & apricots: Energy 323kcal/1356kJ; Protein 10.3g; Carbohydrate 68g, of which sugars 19.5g; Fat 2.1g, of which saturates 0.2g; Cholesterol 0mg; Calcium 107mg; Fibre 3.6g; Sodium 42mg

Bulgur Wheat & Tomato Salad

This appetizing salad is ideal served with fresh crusty bread and home-made chutney or pickle.

Serves 6
350g/12oz/2 cups bulgur wheat
225g/8oz frozen broad (fava) beans
115g/4oz/1 cup frozen petits pois (baby peas)
225g/8oz cherry tomatoes, halved
1 sweet onion, chopped
1 red (bell) pepper, seeded and diced
50g/2oz mangetouts (snow peas), chopped
50g/2oz watercress
45ml/3 tbsp chopped fresh herbs, such as parsley, basil and thyme

For the dressing
75ml/5 tbsp olive oil
15ml/1 tbsp white wine vinegar
5ml/1 tsp mustard powder
salt and ground black pepper

1 Put the bulgur wheat into a large bowl. Add enough cold water to come 2.5cm/1in above the level of the wheat. Leave to soak for approximately 30 minutes.

2 Turn the soaked bulgur wheat into a sieve (strainer) lined with a clean dish towel. Drain the wheat well and use the dish towel to squeeze out any excess water.

3 Cook the broad beans and petits pois in a pan of boiling water for about 3 minutes, until tender. Drain thoroughly. M

4 Mix the beans and peas with the bulgur wheat in a bowl.

5 Add the cherry tomatoes, onion, pepper, mangetouts and watercress to the bulgur wheat mixture and mix. Combine all the ingredients for the dressing, season and stir well.

6 Add the herbs to the salad, season and add enough dressing to taste. Toss the ingredients together.

7 Serve immediately or cover and chill in the refrigerator before serving.

Grilled Aubergine & Couscous Salad

Easy to make, yet packed with Mediterranean flavours, this delicious couscous salad is wonderful served with a crisp green salad.

Serves 2
1 large aubergine (eggplant)
30ml/2 tbsp olive oil
115g/4oz packet garlic and coriander (cilantro) flavoured couscous
30ml/2 tbsp chopped fresh mint
salt and ground black pepper
fresh mint leaves, to garnish

1 Preheat the grill (broiler) to high. Cut the aubergine into large chunky pieces and toss them with the olive oil. Season with salt and ground black pepper to taste and spread the aubergine pieces on a non-stick baking sheet. Grill (broil) for 5–6 minutes, turning occasionally, until golden brown.

2 Meanwhile, prepare the couscous in boiling water, according to the instructions on the packet.

3 Stir the grilled aubergine and chopped mint into the couscous, toss the salad thoroughly to spread the flavours, and serve immediately, garnished with mint leaves.

Cook's Tip
Packets of flavoured couscous are available in most supermarkets – you can use whichever you like, but garlic and coriander (cilantro) is particularly good for this recipe.

Variation
A similar dish, which is also popular around Greece, uses grilled (broiled) courgettes (zucchini) instead of, or as well as, the aubergine. Slice the courgettes into thin rounds or ovals, brush with olive oil, and place under a hot grill (broiler) for a few minutes on each side.

Bulgur wheat & tomato salad: Energy 302kcal/1261kJ; Protein 9.8g; Carbohydrate 42.8g, of which sugars 4.9g; Fat 10.8g, of which saturates 1.5g; Cholesterol 0mg; Calcium 84mg; Fibre 5g; Sodium 17mg
Grilled aubergine & couscous salad: Energy 248kcal/1033kJ; Protein 4.4g; Carbohydrate 32.3g, of which sugars 2.5g; Fat 12.1g, of which saturates 1.7g; Cholesterol 0mg; Calcium 24mg; Fibre 2.5g; Sodium 3mg

Fennel & Egg Tabbouleh with Herbs

This Middle-Eastern classic is given a different twist with the addition of aniseed-flavoured fennel and tangy black olives.

Serves 4

250g/9oz/1 cup bulgur wheat
4 small eggs
1 fennel bulb
1 bunch of spring onions (scallions), chopped
25g/1oz/½ cup drained sun-dried tomatoes in oil, sliced
45ml/3 tbsp chopped fresh parsley
30ml/2 tbsp chopped fresh mint
75g/3oz/½ cup black olives
60ml/4 tbsp olive oil
30ml/2 tbsp garlic oil
30ml/2 tbsp lemon juice
50g/2oz/½ cup chopped hazelnuts, toasted
1 open-textured loaf or 4 pitta breads, warmed
salt and ground black pepper

1 Put the bulgur wheat into a large bowl. Add enough cold water to come 2.5cm/1in above the level of the wheat. Leave to soak for approximately 30 minutes.

2 Turn the soaked bulgur wheat into a sieve (strainer) lined with a clean dish towel. Drain the wheat well and use the dish towel to squeeze out any excess water. Leave to cool.

3 Cook the eggs in boiling water for 8 minutes. Cool under running water, peel and quarter.

4 Halve and finely slice the fennel. Boil in salted water for 6 minutes, then drain and cool under running water. Drain again thoroughly.

5 Combine the eggs, fennel, spring onions, sun-dried tomatoes, parsley, mint and olives with the bulgur wheat.

6 Put the olive oil, garlic oil and lemon juice in a small bowl and whisk together with a fork. Add to the bulgur wheat salad, toss well, then add the nuts. Season with salt and pepper to taste, then tear the bread into pieces and add to the salad. Serve the salad immediately.

Chargrilled Pepper Salad with Pesto

The ingredients of this colourful salad are simple and few, but the overall flavour is quite intense.

Serves 4

1 large red (bell) pepper, halved and seeded
1 large green (bell) pepper, halved and seeded
250g/9oz/2¼ cups dried fusilli tricolore or other pasta shapes
1 handful fresh basil leaves
1 handful fresh coriander (cilantro) leaves
1 garlic clove
salt and ground black pepper

For the dressing

30ml/2 tbsp pesto
juice of ½ lemon
60ml/4 tbsp extra-virgin olive oil

1 Place the red and green pepper halves, skin-side up, on a grill (broiler) rack and grill (broil) until the skins have blistered and are beginning to char. Transfer the peppers to a bowl, cover with crumpled kitchen paper and leave to cool slightly. When they are cool enough to handle, rub off the skins and discard.

2 Bring a large pan of salted water to the boil, add the pasta and cook according to the packet instructions, until al dente.

3 Meanwhile, whisk together the pesto, lemon juice and olive oil in a large bowl. Season to taste with salt and pepper.

4 Drain the cooked pasta well and add to the bowl of dressing. Toss thoroughly to mix and set aside to cool.

5 Chop the pepper flesh and add to the pasta. Put most of the basil and coriander and all the garlic on a board and chop them. Add the herb mixture to the pasta and toss, then season to taste, if necessary, and serve, garnished with the herb leaves.

Cook's Tip

Serve the salad at room temperature or lightly chilled, whichever you prefer.

Fennel & egg tabbouleh with herbs: Energy 842kcal/3521kJ; Protein 25g; Carbohydrate 106g, of which sugars 5.7g; Fat 37.6g, of which saturates 5.5g; Cholesterol 190mg; Calcium 273mg; Fibre 6g; Sodium 946mg
Chargrilled pepper salad: Energy 379kcal/1593kJ; Protein 11.7g; Carbohydrate 52.3g, of which sugars 7.7g; Fat 15.1g, of which saturates 3.3g; Cholesterol 8mg; Calcium 138mg; Fibre 3.9g; Sodium 91mg

Roasted Tomato & Rocket Salad

This is a good side salad to accompany a cheese flan or a fresh herb pizza.

Serves 4

450g/1lb ripe baby Italian plum tomatoes, halved lengthwise
75ml/5 tbsp extra-virgin olive oil
2 garlic cloves, cut into thin slivers
225g/8oz/2 cups dried pasta shapes
30ml/2 tbsp balsamic vinegar
2 pieces sun-dried tomato in olive oil, drained and chopped
large pinch of sugar
1 handful rocket (arugula) leaves
salt and ground black pepper

1 Preheat the oven to 190°C/375°F/Gas 5. Arrange the halved tomatoes, cut side up, in a roasting pan. Drizzle 30ml/2 tbsp of the oil over them and sprinkle with the slivers of garlic and salt and pepper to taste. Roast for 20 minutes, turning once.

2 Meanwhile, bring a large pan of lightly salted water to the boil, add the pasta and cook according to the packet instructions, until it is al dente.

3 Put the remaining oil in a large bowl with the balsamic vinegar, sun-dried tomatoes and sugar with salt and ground black pepper to taste.

4 Drain the pasta, add it to the bowl of dressing and toss to mix. Add the roasted tomatoes and mix gently.

5 Just before serving, add the rocket leaves, toss lightly and taste for seasoning. Serve at room temperature or chilled.

Variations

• *If you are in a hurry and don't have time to roast the tomatoes, you can make the salad with halved raw tomatoes instead, but make sure that they are really ripe.*
• *If you like, add 150g/5oz mozzarella cheese, drained and diced, with the rocket.*

Pasta Salad with Cherry Tomatoes

Colourful, tasty and nutritious, this is the ideal pasta salad for a summer picnic, and makes the most of the deliciously sweet cherry tomatoes available in the markets.

Serves 6

300g/11oz/2¾ cups dried fusilli or other pasta shapes
150g/5oz green beans, cut into 5cm/2in lengths
1 potato, about 150g/5oz, diced into small pieces
200g/7oz cherry tomatoes, halved
2 spring onions (scallions), finely chopped or 90g/3½oz white of leek, finely chopped
90g/3½oz Parmesan cheese, diced or coarsely shaved
6–8 pitted black olives, cut into rings
15–30ml/1–2 tbsp capers, to taste

For the dressing

90ml/6 tbsp extra-virgin olive oil
15ml/1 tbsp balsamic vinegar
15ml/1 tbsp chopped fresh flat leaf parsley
salt and ground black pepper

1 Bring a large pan of salted water to the boil, add the pasta and cook according to the packet instructions, until al dente.

2 Drain, cool and rinse under cold water, then shake the colander to remove as much water as possible. Leave to drain and dry.

3 Cook the beans and diced potato in a pan of salted boiling water for 5–6 minutes, or until tender. Drain and leave the vegetables to cool.

4 To make the dressing, put olive oil, balsamic vinegar and parsley in a large serving bowl with salt and pepper to taste and whisk well to mix.

5 Add the cherry tomatoes, spring onions or leek, Parmesan, olive rings and capers to the dressing, then the cold pasta, beans and potato. Toss well to mix.

6 Cover and leave to stand for about 30 minutes. Taste the salad and adjust the seasoning before serving.

Roasted tomato & rocket salad: Energy 339kcal/1427kJ; Protein 7.9g; Carbohydrate 45.5g, of which sugars 5.6g; Fat 15.3g, of which saturates 2.2g; Cholesterol 0mg; Calcium 47mg; Fibre 3.4g; Sodium 16mg
Pasta salad: Energy 388kcal/1625kJ; Protein 13.5g; Carbohydrate 43.4g, of which sugars 4g; Fat 19g, of which saturates 5.1g; Cholesterol 15mg; Calcium 221mg; Fibre 3.3g; Sodium 547mg

Summer Salad

Ripe red tomatoes, mozzarella and olives make a good base for a fresh and tangy salad that is perfect for a light summer lunch.

Serves 4

350g/12oz/3 cups dried penne or other pasta shapes
150g/5oz packet mozzarella di bufala, drained and diced
3 ripe tomatoes, diced
10 pitted black olives, sliced
10 pitted green olives, sliced
1 spring onion (scallion), thinly sliced on the diagonal
1 handful fresh basil leaves

For the dressing

90ml/6 tbsp extra virgin olive oil
15ml/1 tbsp balsamic vinegar or lemon juice
salt and ground black pepper

1 Bring a large pan of salted water to the boil, add the pasta and cook according to the packet instructions, until al dente.

2 Drain and rinse under cold running water, then drain thoroughly again. Leave the pasta to drain.

3 To make the dressing, whisk the olive oil and balsamic vinegar or lemon juice in a large bowl with a little salt and pepper.

4 Add the pasta, mozzarella, tomatoes, olives and spring onion to the dressing and toss together well. Adjust the seasoning and garnish with basil before serving.

Variation

Make the salad more substantial by adding other ingredients, such as sliced peppers, toasted pine nuts, canned artichoke hearts, baby corn cobs – whatever you have to hand.

Cook's Tip

Mozzarella made from buffalo milk has more flavour than the type made with cow's milk. It is now widely available.

Pepper & Mushroom Pasta Salad

A combination of grilled peppers and two different kinds of mushroom makes this salad colourful as well as nutritious. Serve with chunks of ciabatta or a flavoured focaccia for a scrumptious meal.

Serves 6

1 red (bell) pepper, halved
1 yellow (bell) pepper, halved
1 green (bell) pepper, halved
350g/12oz dried whole-wheat pasta shells or fusilli
30ml/2 tbsp olive oil
45ml/3 tbsp balsamic vinegar
75ml/5 tbsp tomato juice
30ml/2 tbsp chopped fresh basil
15ml/1 tbsp chopped fresh thyme
175g/6oz/2¼ cups shiitake mushrooms, diced
175g/6oz/2¼ cups oyster mushrooms, sliced
400g/14oz can black-eyed beans (peas), drained and rinsed
115g/4oz/¾ cup sultanas (golden raisins)
2 bunches spring onions (scallions), finely chopped
salt and ground black pepper

1 Preheat the grill (broiler) to hot. Put the peppers cut side down on a grill pan rack and place under the grill for 10–15 minutes, until the skins are charred. Put in a bowl, cover crumpled kitchen paper and set aside to cool.

2 Meanwhile, bring a large pan of lightly salted water to the boil, add the pasta and cook according to the packet instructions, until al dente. Drain thoroughly.

3 Mix together the oil, vinegar, tomato juice, basil and thyme, add to the warm pasta and toss.

4 Remove and discard the skins from the peppers. Seed and slice and add to the pasta.

5 Add the mushrooms, beans, sultanas and spring onions to the pasta and season with salt and pepper to taste.

6 Toss the ingredients to mix and serve immediately. Alternatively, cover and chill in the refrigerator before serving.

Summer salad: Energy 635kcal/2658kJ; Protein 18.7g; Carbohydrate 67.2g, of which sugars 5.3g; Fat 34.2g, of which saturates 9.1g; Cholesterol 22mg; Calcium 210mg; Fibre 5.5g; Sodium 1845mg
Pepper & mushroom pasta salad: Energy 390kcal/1650kJ; Protein 15.6g; Carbohydrate 71.8g, of which sugars 25.4g; Fat 6.5g, of which saturates 1g; Cholesterol 0mg; Calcium 126mg; Fibre 12.5g; Sodium 380mg

Whole-wheat Pasta Salad

This substantial vegetarian salad is easily assembled from any combination of seasonal vegetables. Use raw or lightly blanched vegetables, or a mixture of both to ring the changes.

Serves 8

450g/1lb dried whole-wheat pasta, such as fusilli or penne
45ml/3 tbsp olive oil
2 carrots
1 small head broccoli, halved
115g/4oz/1 cup shelled peas, fresh or frozen
1 red or yellow (bell) pepper, halved and seeded
2 celery stalks
4 spring onions (scallions)
1 large tomato
50g/2oz/½ cup pitted olives, halved
75g/3oz/⅔ cup diced Cheddar or mozzarella, or a combination

For the dressing

45ml/3 tbsp balsamic or wine vinegar
60ml/4 tbsp olive oil
15ml/1 tbsp Dijon mustard
15ml/1 tbsp sesame seeds
10ml/2 tsp finely chopped mixed fresh herbs, such as parsley, thyme and basil
salt and ground black pepper

1 Bring a large pan of salted water to the boil, add the pasta and cook according to the packet instructions, until al dente. Drain, and rinse under cold water to stop the cooking. Drain well and turn into a large bowl. Toss with the olive oil and allow to cool completely.

2 Lightly blanch the carrots, broccoli and peas in a large pan of boiling water. Refresh under cold water. Drain well.

3 Chop the carrots and broccoli into bitesize pieces and add to the pasta with the peas. Slice the pepper, celery, spring onions and tomato into small pieces. Add them to the salad with the olives.

4 To make the dressing, whisk the vinegar with the oil and mustard in a small bowl. Stir in the sesame seeds and herbs and season with salt and pepper. Whisk well to combine, then pour over the salad. Toss to mix, then stir in the cheese. Leave to stand for 15 minutes before serving.

Pasta, Asparagus & Potato Salad

Made with whole-wheat pasta, this delicious salad is a real treat, especially when made with fresh asparagus just in season.

Serves 4

225g/8oz/2 cups dried whole-wheat pasta shapes
60ml/4 tbsp extra virgin olive oil
350g/12oz baby new potatoes
225g/8oz asparagus
115g/4oz piece Parmesan cheese
salt and ground black pepper

1 Bring a large pan of salted water to the boil, add the pasta and cook according to the packet instructions, until al dente.

2 Drain well and toss with the olive oil while the pasta is still warm. Season with salt and ground black pepper.

3 Cook the potatoes in boiling salted water for 15 minutes, or until tender. Drain and toss together with the pasta.

4 Trim any woody ends off the asparagus and halve the stalks if they are very long.

5 Blanch the asparagus in boiling salted water for 6 minutes, until bright green and still crunchy. Drain, then plunge into cold water to refresh. Drain and dry on kitchen paper.

6 Toss the asparagus with the potatoes and pasta, adjust the seasoning to taste and transfer to a shallow serving bowl.

7 Using a vegetable peeler, shave the Parmesan over the salad.

Cook's Tip

Asparagus takes 3 years to grow from seed to crop, which may account for its expense. Trim off the woody ends before use. It is a rich source of vitamin C. Store asparagus in the salad drawer of the refrigerator and eat within 2–3 days.

Whole-wheat pasta salad: Energy 374kcal/1569kJ; Protein 14g; Carbohydrate 43.7g, of which sugars 6.9g; Fat 16.9g, of which saturates 4.1g; Cholesterol 9mg; Calcium 145mg; Fibre 8.1g; Sodium 354mg
Pasta, asparagus & potato salad: Energy 487kcal/2042kJ; Protein 22g; Carbohydrate 52.5g, of which sugars 4.3g; Fat 22.4g, of which saturates 7.8g; Cholesterol 29mg; Calcium 383mg; Fibre 6.6g; Sodium 397mg

Pasta Salad with Olives

This delicious salad combines all the flavours of the Mediterranean. It is an excellent way of serving pasta and is particularly nice on hot summer days.

Serves 6

450g/1lb/4 cups dried pasta shapes, such as shells, farfalle or penne
60ml/4 tbsp extra virgin olive oil
10 sun-dried tomatoes, thinly sliced
30ml/2 tbsp capers, in brine or salted
75g/3oz/⅔ cup black olives, pitted
2 garlic cloves, finely chopped
45ml/3 tbsp balsamic vinegar
45ml/3 tbsp chopped fresh parsley
salt and ground black pepper

1 Bring a large pan of salted water to the boil, add the pasta and cook according to the packet instructions, until al dente. Drain, and rinse under cold water. Drain well and turn into a large bowl. Toss with the olive oil and set aside.

2 Soak the tomatoes in a bowl of hot water for 10 minutes, then drain, reserving the soaking liquid. Rinse the capers well. If they have been preserved in salt, soak them in a little hot water for10 minutes. Rinse again.

3 Combine the olives, tomatoes, capers, garlic and vinegar in a small bowl. Season with salt and pepper.

4 Stir the vegetable mixture into the pasta and toss well. Add 30–45ml/2–3 tbsp of the tomato water if the salad seems too dry. Toss with parsley and leave the salad to stand for 15 minutes before serving.

Variations

- *You could use green olives instead of the black variety to ring the changes.*
- *Pimiento stuffed olives would add extra colour.*
- *Add chopped fresh tomatoes to enhance the tomato flavour.*

Pasta, Olive & Avocado Salad

The ingredients of this salad are united by a wonderful sun-dried tomato and fresh basil dressing.

Serves 6

225g/8oz/2 cups dried fusilli pasta or other pasta shapes
115g/4oz can corn, drained, or frozen corn, thawed
½ red (bell) pepper, seeded and diced
8 black olives, pitted and sliced
3 spring onions (scallions), finely chopped
2 medium avocados
15ml/1 tbsp lemon juice

For the dressing

2 sun-dried tomato halves, loose-packed (not preserved in oil)
25ml/1½ tbsp balsamic or white wine vinegar
25ml/1½ tbsp red wine vinegar
½ garlic clove, crushed
2.5ml/½ tsp salt
75ml/5 tbsp olive oil
15ml/1 tbsp sliced fresh basil

1 To make the dressing, drop the sun-dried tomatoes into a pan containing 2.5cm/1in boiling water and simmer for about 3 minutes until tender. Drain and chop finely.

2 Combine the sun-dried tomatoes, both vinegars, garlic and salt in a food processor. With the machine running, add the olive oil in a stream. Stir in the basil.

3 Bring a large pan of salted water to the boil, add the pasta and cook according to the packet instructions, until al dente. Drain, and rinse under cold water. Drain well.

4 In a large bowl, combine the pasta, drained corn, diced red pepper, olives and spring onions. Add the dressing and toss well to coat thoroughly.

5 Just before serving, peel and stone (pit) the avocados and cut the flesh into cubes. Sprinkle with the lemon juice to stop the flesh from discolouring.

6 Mix the avocado gently into the pasta, then transfer the salad to a serving dish. Serve at room temperature.

Pasta salad: Energy 341kcal/1440kJ; Protein 9.5g; Carbohydrate 56.3g, of which sugars 3.2g; Fat 10.2g, of which saturates 1.4g; Cholesterol 0mg; Calcium 44mg; Fibre 3.1g; Sodium 288mg
Pasta, olive & avocado salad: Energy 329kcal/1374kJ; Protein 6.5g; Carbohydrate 31.1g, of which sugars 3.7g; Fat 20.6g, of which saturates 3.6g; Cholesterol 0mg; Calcium 26mg; Fibre 3.9g; Sodium 412m

Vegetable Pasta Salad

A colourful medley of crisp vegetables, tossed with freshly cooked pasta, makes an ideal light lunch or simple supper.

Serves 4

225g/8oz/2 cups dried pasta shapes
25g/1oz/2 tbsp butter
45ml/3 tbsp extra virgin olive oil
1 small leek, thinly sliced
2 carrots, diced
2.5ml/½ tsp sugar
1 courgette (zucchini), diced
75g/3oz green beans, cut into 2cm/¾in lengths
75g/3oz fresh or frozen peas
1 handful fresh flat leaf parsley, finely chopped
2 ripe Italian plum tomatoes, chopped
salt and ground black pepper

1 Bring a large pan of salted water to the boil, add the pasta and cook according to the packet instructions, until al dente.

2 Meanwhile, heat the butter and oil in a pan. When the mixture sizzles, add the sliced leek and diced carrots.

3 Sprinkle the sugar over and cook, stirring frequently, for about 5 minutes.

4 Stir in the courgette, green beans, peas and plenty of salt and ground black pepper.

5 Cover and cook over a low to medium heat for 5–8 minutes until the vegetables are tender, stirring occasionally.

6 Stir in the parsley and chopped plum tomatoes.

7 Drain the pasta, add the vegetables, then toss to combine.

Cook's Tip
Vary the vegetables according to what is in season and what you have available. Keep them crisp to retain maximum nutritional value.

Roasted Vegetable Pasta Salad

Nothing could be simpler – or more delicious – than tossing freshly cooked pasta with roasted vegetables. The flavour is superb.

Serves 6

1 red (bell) pepper, seeded and cut into 1cm/½in squares
1 yellow or orange (bell) pepper, seeded and cut into 1cm/½in squares
1 small aubergine (eggplant), roughly diced
2 courgettes (zucchini), sliced
75ml/5 tbsp extra virgin olive oil
15ml/1 tbsp chopped fresh flat leaf parsley
5ml/1 tsp dried oregano or marjoram
250g/9oz baby Italian plum tomatoes, hulled and halved lengthwise
2 garlic cloves, roughly chopped
350–400g/12–14oz/3–3½ cups dried pasta shells
salt and ground black pepper
4–6 fresh marjoram or oregano flowers, to garnish

1 Preheat the oven to 190°C/375°F/Gas 5. Rinse the prepared peppers, aubergine and courgettes under cold running water, then drain. Transfer the vegetables to a large roasting pan.

2 Pour 45ml/3 tbsp of the olive oil over the vegetables and sprinkle with the fresh and dried herbs. Add salt and pepper to taste and stir well. Roast for about 30 minutes, stirring two or three times.

3 Stir the halved tomatoes and chopped garlic into the vegetable mixture, then roast for 20 minutes more, stirring once or twice during the cooking time.

4 Meanwhile, bring a large pan of salted water to the boil, add the pasta and cook according to the instructions on the packet, or until *al dente*.

5 Drain the pasta and transfer it to a warmed bowl. Add the roasted vegetables and the remaining oil and toss well.

6 Serve the pasta and vegetables hot in warmed bowls, sprinkling each portion with a few herb flowers.

Vegetable pasta salad: Energy 201kcal/829kJ; Protein 5.5g; Carbohydrate 12g, of which sugars 7.2g; Fat 14.8g, of which saturates 4.7g; Cholesterol 13mg; Calcium 68mg; Fibre 5.5g; Sodium 57mg
Roasted vegetable salad: Energy 319kcal/1343kJ; Protein 8.8g; Carbohydrate 49.6g, of which sugars 8g; Fat 10.8g, of which saturates 1.6g; Cholesterol 0mg; Calcium 34mg; Fibre 4g; Sodium 9mg

Sweet & Hot Vegetable Noodles

This noodle dish has the colour of fire, but only the mildest suggestion of heat.

Serves 4

130g/4½oz dried rice noodles
30ml/2 tbsp groundnut (peanut) oil
2.5cm/1in piece fresh root ginger, sliced into thin batons
1 garlic clove, crushed
130g/4½oz drained canned bamboo shoots, cut into batons
2 carrots, sliced into batons
130g/4½oz/1½ cups beansprouts
1 small white cabbage, shredded
30ml/2 tbsp soy sauce
30ml/2 tbsp plum sauce
10ml/2 tsp sesame oil
15ml/1 tbsp palm sugar (jaggery) or light muscovado (brown) sugar
juice of ½ lime
90g/3½oz mooli (daikon), sliced into thin batons
small bunch fresh coriander (cilantro), chopped
60ml/4 tbsp sesame seeds, toasted

1 Cook the noodles in a large pan of boiling water, following the instructions on the packet.

2 Heat the oil in a wok or large pan and stir-fry the ginger and garlic for 2–3 minutes on a medium heat, until golden.

3 Drain the noodles and set them aside. Add the bamboo shoots to the wok, increase the heat to high and stir-fry for 5 minutes.

4 Add the carrots, beansprouts and cabbage and stir-fry for a further 5 minutes, until they are beginning to char.

5 Stir in the sauces, sesame oil, sugar and lime juice. Add the mooli and coriander, toss to mix, then spoon into a warmed bowl, sprinkle with sesame seeds and serve immediately.

Cook's Tip
Use a large, sharp knife for shredding cabbage. Remove tough outer leaves, then cut into quarters. Cut off the hard core from each quarter, then place flat side down and slice into shreds.

Fried Tofu & Rice Noodle Salad

A light and refreshing salad, this is a meal in itself. Extremely easy to assemble, it is excellent as a last-minute supper dish.

Serves 4

200g/7oz cellophane noodles
8 spring onions (scallions), thinly sliced
300g/11oz marinated deep-fried tofu
about 2.5ml/½ tsp dried chilli flakes
grated rind and juice of 1 lemon
5cm/2in piece fresh root ginger, sliced into fine batons (optional)
1 bunch fresh coriander (cilantro) or parsley, chopped
about 30ml/2 tbsp soy sauce
30ml/2 tbsp toasted sesame oil
65g/2½oz/½ cup sesame or sunflower seeds, toasted, or 75g/3oz/¾ cup peanuts

1 Cover the noodles with boiling water, leave for 5–10 minutes, or according to the packet instructions, then drain and rinse under cold running water. Place in a large bowl.

2 Add the spring onions, tofu and chilli flakes to the noodles, together with the lemon rind and juice, ginger, if using, coriander, soy sauce, sesame oil and seeds or nuts. Toss together, then add salt and pepper to taste and serve.

Cook's Tip
Made from bean curd, tofu is a good source of protein for vegetarians. It is bland in taste but absorbs marinades well.

Variations
- *Try making a thin egg omelette seasoned with soy sauce and a pinch of sugar then rolled up and finely sliced. Use with or instead of the marinated tofu.*
- *Peanuts could be toasted and chopped and used instead of the sesame or sunflower seeds.*
- *Green beans or mangetouts (snow peas) can be blanched and used with or instead of the coriander (cilantro).*

Sweet & hot vegetable noodles: Energy 368kcal/1530kJ; Protein 8.8g; Carbohydrate 45.8g, of which sugars 17.6g; Fat 16.5g, of which saturates 2.3g; Cholesterol 0mg; Calcium 200mg; Fibre 6.2g; Sodium 650mg
Fried tofu & rice noodle salad: Energy 699kcal/2898kJ; Protein 23.7g; Carbohydrate 43.6g, of which sugars 1.9g; Fat 47.1g, of which saturates 5.7g; Cholesterol 0mg; Calcium 1235mg; Fibre 1.6g; Sodium 554mg

Pineapple, Ginger & Chilli Noodles

Fragrant and fruity, this noodle dish makes an exotic change from pasta. The pineapple is glazed to give a delicious sweetness, while garlic and chilli add a contrasting savoury note.

Serves 4

275g/10oz dried udon noodles
½ pineapple, peeled, cored and sliced into 4cm/1½in rings
45ml/3 tbsp soft light brown sugar
60ml/4 tbsp fresh lime juice
60ml/4 tbsp coconut milk
30ml/2 tbsp grated fresh root ginger
2 garlic cloves, finely chopped
1 ripe mango or 2 peaches, finely diced
freshly ground black pepper

For the garnish

2 spring onions (scallions), finely sliced
2 red chillies, seeded and finely shredded
fresh mint leaves

1 Cook the noodles in a large pan of boiling water until tender, according to the instructions on the packet. Drain, refresh under cold water and drain again.

2 Place the pineapple rings on a flameproof dish, sprinkle with 30ml/2 tbsp of the sugar and grill (broil) for about 5 minutes or until golden. Cool slightly and cut into small dice.

3 Mix the lime juice and coconut milk in a salad bowl. Add the remaining brown sugar, with the fresh root ginger and garlic, and whisk well.

4 Add the noodles and pineapple. Add the mango or peaches and toss. Scatter over the spring onions, chillies and mint leaves before serving.

Cook's Tip

The Japanese udon noodles are made from wheat flour. They are white and are usually fairly thick with a slightly chewy texture. They are often used in soups and are eaten hot or cold.

Hot & Sour Noodle Salad

Noodles make the perfect basis for a salad, absorbing the dressing and providing a contrast in texture to the crisp vegetables.

Serves 2

200g/7oz dried thin rice noodles
1 small bunch fresh coriander (cilantro)
2 tomatoes, seeded and sliced
130g/4½oz baby corn cobs, sliced
4 spring onions (scallions), thinly sliced
1 red (bell) pepper, seeded and finely chopped
juice of 2 limes
2 small fresh green chillies, seeded and finely chopped
10ml/2 tsp sugar
115g/4oz/1 cup peanuts, toasted and chopped
30ml/2 tbsp soy sauce
salt

1 Bring a large pan of lightly salted water to the boil. Snap the noodles into short lengths, add to the pan and cook for 3–4 minutes. Drain, then rinse under cold water and drain again.

2 Set aside a few coriander leaves for the garnish. Chop the remaining leaves and place them in a large serving bowl.

3 Put the noodles into the bowl with the chopped coriander. Add the tomato slices, corn cobs, spring onions, red pepper, lime juice, chillies, sugar and toasted peanuts.

4 Season with the soy sauce, then taste and add a little salt if you think the mixture needs it.

5 Toss the salad lightly but thoroughly, then garnish with the reserved coriander leaves and serve immediately.

Variation

If you are not a fan of the strong taste of coriander (cilantro), try swapping in Thai basil for this recipe. It has a subtle, yet distinctive flavour that complements chilli and lime juice well. Thai basil is now available as a fresh herb in many Oriental markets and supermarkets.

Pineapple, ginger & chilli noodles: Energy 380kcal/1604kJ; Protein 4.5g; Carbohydrate 89.4g, of which sugars 33.1g; Fat 0.5g, of which saturates 0.1g; Cholesterol 0mg; Calcium 48mg; Fibre 3.2g; Sodium 29mg
Hot & sour noodle salad: Energy 783kcal/3269kJ; Protein 24.7g; Carbohydrate 106.4g, of which sugars 20.4g; Fat 27.9g, of which saturates 5.2g; Cholesterol 0mg; Calcium 129mg; Fibre 8.5g; Sodium 1845mg

Rice Noodles with Crunchy Vegetables and Fresh Herbs

Rice noodles simply tossed with crunchy salad vegetables, fresh herbs and sharp flavourings make a delicious and satisfying vegetarian snack.

Serves 4
half a small cucumber
4–6 lettuce leaves
1 bunch mixed fresh basil, coriander (cilantro), mint and oregano
225g/8oz dried rice sticks (vermicelli)
115g/4oz/½ cup beansprouts
juice of half a lime
soy sauce, to drizzle (optional)

1 Peel the cucumber, cut it in half lengthwise, remove the seeds, and cut into matchsticks.

2 Using a sharp knife, cut the lettuce into fine shreds.

3 Remove the stalks from the herbs and shred the leaves.

4 Add the rice sticks to a pan of boiling water, loosening them gently, and cook for 3–4 minutes, or until white and just tender. Drain, rinse under cold water, and drain again.

5 In a bowl, toss the shredded lettuce, beansprouts and cucumber together, then toss in the shredded herbs.

6 Add the noodles and lime juice and toss together.

7 Drizzle with a little soy sauce, if using, and serve immediately.

Cook's Tip
Rice noodles come in various widths, from very thin strands known as rice vermicelli, which are popular in Thailand and Southern China, to thicker rice sticks, which are used in Vietnam and Malaysia.

Thai Noodle Salad

The addition of coconut milk and sesame oil gives an unusual nutty flavour to the dressing for this colourful noodle salad.

Serves 4–6
350g/12oz somen noodles
1 large carrot, cut into thin strips
1 bunch asparagus, trimmed and cut into 4cm/1½in lengths
1 red (bell) pepper, seeded and cut into fine strips
115g/4oz mangetouts (snow peas), topped, tailed and halved
115g/4oz baby corn cobs, halved lengthwise
115g/4oz beansprouts
115g/4oz can water chestnuts, drained and finely sliced
1 lime, cut into wedges, 50g/2oz/½ cup roasted peanuts, roughly chopped, and fresh coriander (cilantro) leaves, to garnish

For the dressing
45ml/3 tbsp roughly torn fresh basil
75ml/5 tbsp roughly chopped fresh mint
250ml/8fl oz/1 cup coconut milk
30ml/2 tbsp dark sesame oil
15ml/1 tbsp grated fresh root ginger
2 garlic cloves, finely chopped
juice of 1 lime
2 spring onions (scallions), finely chopped
salt and cayenne pepper

1 To make the dressing, combine the herbs, coconut milk, sesame oil, ginger, garlic, lime juice and spring onions in a large bowl and mix well. Season to taste with salt and cayenne pepper.

2 Cook the noodles in a pan of boiling water, according to the instructions on the packet, until just tender. Drain, rinse under cold running water and drain again.

3 Cook all the vegetables, except the water chestnuts, in separate pans of boiling, lightly salted water until they are tender but still crisp. Drain, plunge them immediately into cold water and drain again.

4 Toss the noodles, vegetables, water chestnuts and dressing together. Arrange on individual serving plates and garnish the salads with the lime wedges, chopped peanuts and coriander.

Rice noodles with fresh herbs: Energy 217kcal/908kJ; Protein 6.4g; Carbohydrate 46.1g, of which sugars 1.5g; Fat 0.6g, of which saturates 0.1g; Cholesterol 0mg; Calcium 51mg; Fibre 1.3g; Sodium 11mg
Thai noodle salad: Energy 365kcal/1521kJ; Protein 6g; Carbohydrate 55.1g, of which sugars 6.7g; Fat 12.8g, of which saturates 2.3g; Cholesterol 0mg; Calcium 61mg; Fibre 2.5g; Sodium 280mg

Sesame Noodle Salad with Hot Peanuts

An Eastern-inspired salad with crunchy vegetables and a light soy dressing. The hot peanuts make a surprisingly successful union with the cold noodles.

Serves 4

350g/12oz egg noodles
2 carrots, cut into fine julienne strips
½ cucumber, peeled, seeded and cut into 1cm/½in cubes
115g/4oz celeriac, peeled and cut into fine julienne strips
6 spring onions (scallions), finely sliced
8 canned water chestnuts, drained and finely sliced
175g/6oz/1⅔ cups beansprouts
1 small fresh green chilli, seeded and finely chopped
30ml/2 tbsp sesame seeds and 115g/4oz/1 cup peanuts, to serve

For the dressing

15ml/1 tbsp dark soy sauce
15ml/1 tbsp light soy sauce
15ml/1 tbsp clear honey
15ml/1 tbsp Chinese rice wine or dry sherry
15ml/1 tbsp sesame oil

1 Cook the egg noodles in boiling water, according to the instructions on the packet.

2 Drain the noodles, refresh in cold water, then drain again. Mix the noodles together with all of the prepared vegetables. Preheat the oven to 200°C/400°F/ Gas 6.

3 Combine the dressing ingredients in a small bowl, then toss into the noodle and vegetable mixture. Divide the salad between 4 plates.

4 Place the sesame seeds and peanuts on separate baking trays and place in the oven. Take the sesame seeds out after 5 minutes and continue to cook the peanuts for another 5 minutes until evenly browned.

5 Sprinkle the sesame seeds and peanuts evenly over each salad portion and serve at once.

Sesame Noodle Salad

Toasted sesame oil adds a nutty flavour to this salad, which is at its best when served warm.

Serves 2–4

250g/9oz medium egg noodles
200g/7oz/1¾ cups sugar snap peas or mangetouts (snow peas), sliced diagonally
2 carrots, cut into fine julienne strips
2 tomatoes, seeded and diced
15ml/1 tbsp sesame seeds
30ml/2 tbsp chopped fresh coriander (cilantro), plus coriander sprigs, to garnish
3 spring onions (scallions), shredded

For the dressing

10ml/2 tsp light soy sauce
30ml/2 tbsp toasted sesame seed oil
15ml/1 tbsp sunflower oil
4cm/1½in piece of fresh root ginger, finely grated
1 garlic clove, crushed

1 Bring a large pan of water to the boil, add the noodles and remove the pan from the heat. Cover and leave to stand for about 4 minutes, until the noodles are just tender.

2 Meanwhile, bring a second, smaller pan of water to the boil. Add the sugar snap peas or mangetouts, bring back to the boil and cook for 2 minutes. Drain and refresh under cold water, then drain again.

3 To make the dressing, put the soy sauce, sesame seed and sunflower oils, ginger and garlic in a screw-top jar. Close tightly and shake vigorously to mix.

4 Drain the noodles thoroughly and turn them into a large bowl. Add the peas or mangetouts, carrots, tomatoes and chopped fresh coriander.

5 Pour the dressing over the top, and toss thoroughly with your hands to combine.

6 Sprinkle the salad with the sesame seeds, garnish with the shredded spring onions and coriander sprigs and serve while the noodles are still warm.

Salad with hot peanuts: Energy 467kcal/1967kJ; Protein 14.6g; Carbohydrate 73.3g, of which sugars 10.9g; Fat 14.8g, of which saturates 3.2g; Cholesterol 26mg; Calcium 121mg; Fibre 5.8g; Sodium 728mg
Sesame noodle salad: Energy 386kcal/1622kJ; Protein 10.9g; Carbohydrate 52.9g, of which sugars 8.6g; Fat 16g, of which saturates 3g; Cholesterol 19mg; Calcium 85mg; Fibre 5.1g; Sodium 310mg.

Fresh Fruit Salad

A light and refreshing fruit salad makes a healthy and nutritious end to a meal. The natural fruit sugars are kinder to the body than refined sugars.

Serves 6
2 peaches
2 oranges
2 eating apples
16–20 strawberries
30ml/2 tbsp lemon juice
15–30ml/1–2 tbsp orange flower water
a few fresh mint leaves, to decorate

1 Place the peaches in a bowl and pour over boiling water. Leave to stand for 1 minute, then lift out with a slotted spoon, peel, stone (pit) and cut the flesh into thick slices.

2 Peel the oranges with a sharp knife, removing all the white pith, and segment them, catching any juice in a bowl.

3 Peel and core the apples and cut into thin slices.

4 Using the point of a knife, hull the strawberries and halve or quarter the fruits if they are large.

5 Place all the prepared fruit in a large dish.

6 Blend together the lemon juice, orange flower water and any reserved orange juice.

7 Pour the mixture over the salad and toss lightly. Serve decorated with a few fresh mint leaves.

Cook's Tip
Vary the fruit according to what is in season. A variety of fruits can be used for this salad depending on what is available. You could try adding grapes or sliced pears, or choosing some tropical such as mango or pineapple.

Fragrant Fruit Salad

A medley of colourful and exotic fruit, this fresh-tasting salad is the perfect dessert for a dinner party.

Serves 6
130g/4½oz/scant ¾ cup sugar
thinly pared rind and juice of 1 lime
150ml/¼ pint/⅔ cup water
60ml/4 tbsp brandy
5ml/1 tsp instant coffee granules or powder dissolved in 30ml/2 tbsp boiling water
1 small pineapple
1 papaya
2 pomegranates
1 mango
2 passion fruit or kiwi fruit
strips of lime rind, to decorate

1 Put the sugar and lime rind in a small pan with the water. Heat gently until the sugar dissolves, then bring to the boil and simmer for 5 minutes. Leave to cool, then strain into a large serving bowl, discarding the lime rind. Stir in the lime juice, brandy and dissolved coffee.

2 Using a sharp knife, cut the plume and stalk ends from the pineapple. Cut off the peel, then remove the central core and discard. Slice the flesh into bitesize pieces and add to the bowl.

3 Halve the papaya and scoop out the seeds. Cut away the skin, then slice the papaya. Halve the pomegranates and scoop out the seeds. Add to the bowl.

4 Cut the mango lengthwise into three pieces, along each side of the stone (pit). Peel the skin off the flesh. Cut into chunks and add to the bowl.

5 Halve the passion fruit and scoop out the flesh using a teaspoon, or peel and chop the kiwi fruit. Add to the bowl and serve, decorated with lime rind.

Cook's Tip
Allow the salad to stand at room temperature for 1 hour before serving so that the flavours can blend.

Fresh fruit salad: Energy 29Kcal/163kJ; Protein 0.8g; Carbohydrate 9.3g, of which sugars 9.3g; Fat 0.1g, of which saturates 0g; Cholesterol 0g; Fibre 1.6g; Calcium 10mg; Sodium 0mg
Fragrant fruit salad: Energy 146kcal/620kJ; Protein 1g; Carbohydrate 33.2g, of which sugars 33.2g; Fat 0.3g, of which saturates 0g; Cholesterol 0mg; Calcium 40mg; Fibre 2.9g; Sodium 7mg

Italian Fruit Salad & Ice Cream

Fresh summer fruits are steeped in fruit juice to make a delicious Italian salad, which is delectable on its own, but can also be turned into a wickedly rich ice cream. Serve some of the fruit salad alongside the ice cream for a glorious fruity experience.

Serves 6

900g/2lb mixed summer fruits such as strawberries, raspberries, loganberries, redcurrants, blueberries, peaches, apricots, plums, melons and nectarines
juice of 3–4 oranges
juice of 1 lemon
15ml/1 tbsp liquid pear and apple concentrate
60ml/4 tbsp whipping cream
fresh mint sprigs, to decorate

1 Prepare the fruit according to type and cut into reasonably small pieces. Put the prepared fruit into a serving bowl and pour over enough orange juice to cover. Add the lemon juice and chill for 2 hours.

2 Set half the macerated fruit aside to serve as it is. Purée the remainder in a blender or food processor.

3 Gently warm the pear and apple concentrate and stir into the fruit purée. Whip the cream and fold it in.

4 Churn the mixture in an ice-cream maker. Alternatively, place in a suitable container for freezing. Freeze until ice crystals form around the edge, then beat the mixture until smooth. Repeat the process once or twice, then freeze until firm.

5 Allow to soften slightly in the refrigerator before serving, decorated with sprigs of mint.

Cook's Tip
Add 30ml/2 tbsp orange liqueur to the ice cream or the fruit salad for an added touch of luxury.

Tropical Scented Fruit Salad

With its special colour and exotic flavour, this fresh fruit salad is perfect after a rich, heavy meal. Serve the fruit salad with whipping cream flavoured with a little finely chopped drained preserved stem ginger.

Serves 4–6

6 oranges
350–400g/12–14oz/3–3½ cups strawberries
1–2 passion fruit
120ml/4fl oz/½ cup medium dry or sweet white wine

1 To segment the oranges, cut a slice off the top and bottom of each orange to expose the flesh. Place on a board and remove the skin, cutting downwards. Take care to remove all the white pith. Cut between the membranes to release the orange segments.

2 Using the point of a knife, hull and halve the strawberries.

3 Put the orange segments in a serving bowl with the hulled and halved strawberries.

4 Halve the passion fruit and, using a teaspoon, scoop the flesh into the bowl.

5 Pour the wine over the fruit and toss gently. Cover and chill in the refrigerator until ready to serve.

Variation
Use three small blood oranges and three ordinary oranges.

Cook's tip
Passion fruit is a dark purple, wrinkly egg-shaped fruit, which has a pulpy golden flesh with edible black seeds. To prepare it, cut it in half and scoop out the middle with a spoon. Passion fruit is rich in vitamins A and C.

Italian fruit salad: Energy 69kcal/289kJ; Protein 2.2g; Carbohydrate 15.2g, of which sugars 15.2g; Fat 0.2g, of which saturates 0g; Cholesterol 0mg; Calcium 38mg; Fibre 1.7g; Sodium 18mg
Tropical scented fruit salad: Energy 81kcal/342kJ; Protein 2g; Carbohydrate 15.6g, of which sugars 15.6g; Fat 0.2g, of which saturates 0g; Cholesterol 0mg; Calcium 75mg; Fibre 3g; Sodium 13mg

Iced Fruit Mountain

This dramatic display of fruit arranged on a 'mountain' of ice cubes is bound to delight your guests. Cut the pieces of fruit larger than for a fruit salad and supply cocktail sticks for spearing.

Serves 6–8
1 star fruit
4 kumquats
225g/8oz large strawberries
1 apple and/or 1 Asian pear
2 large orange, peeled
1 Charentais melon and/or ½ watermelon
6 physalis
225g/8oz seedless black grapes
8 fresh lychees, peeled (optional)
caster (superfine) sugar, for dipping
wedges of kaffir lime, to decorate

1 Slice the star fruit and halve the kumquats. Leave the hulls on the strawberries. Cut the apple and/or Asian pear into wedges, and the oranges into segments. Use a melon baller for the melon or, alternatively, cut the melon into neat wedges. Chill all the fruit in the refrigerator.

2 Prepare the ice cube 'mountain'. Choose a wide, shallow bowl that, when turned upside down, will fit neatly on a serving platter. Fill the bowl with crushed ice cubes. Put it in the freezer with the serving platter. Leave in the freezer for at least 1 hour.

3 Remove the serving platter and bowl of ice from the freezer. Invert the serving platter on top of the bowl of ice, then turn platter and bowl over. Lift off the bowl and arrange the pieces of fruit on the ice 'mountain'.

4 Decorate the mountain with the kaffir lime wedges, and serve the fruit at once, handing round a bowl of sugar separately for guests with a sweet tooth.

Variation
Vary the fruit as you wish, but you need a good mix of tropical, citrus and soft fruit for the best effect.

Exotic Fruit Salad

Passion fruit makes a superb dressing for any fruit, but really brings out the flavour of exotic varieties. You can easily double the recipe, then serve the rest for the next day's breakfast.

Serves 6
1 mango
1 papaya
2 kiwi fruit
coconut or vanilla ice cream, to serve

For the dressing
3 passion fruit
thinly pared rind and juice of 1 lime
5ml/1 tsp hazelnut or walnut oil
15ml/1 tbsp clear honey

1 Peel the mango, cut it into three slices, then cut the flesh into chunks and place it in a large bowl.

2 Peel and halve the papaya. Scoop out the seeds. Chop the flesh.

3 Cut both ends off each kiwi fruit, then stand them on a board. Using a small sharp knife, cut off the skin from top to bottom. Cut each kiwi fruit in half lengthwise, then cut into thick slices. Combine all the fruit in a large serving bowl.

4 To make the dressing, cut each passion fruit in half and scoop the seeds out into a strainer set over a small bowl. Press the seeds well to extract all their juices.

5 Lightly whisk the remaining dressing ingredients into the passion fruit juice, then pour the dressing over the prepared fruit in the serving bowl.

6 Mix gently to combine. Leave to chill for 1 hour before serving with scoops of coconut or vanilla ice cream.

Cook's Tip
A clear golden honey scented with orange blossom or acacia blossom would be perfect for the dressing.

Iced fruit mountain: Energy 56kcal/239kJ; Protein 1.1g; Carbohydrate 13.4g, of which sugars 13.4g; Fat 0.2g, of which saturates 0g; Cholesterol 0mg; Calcium 35mg; Fibre 1.7g; Sodium 17mg
Exotic fruit salad: Energy 66kcal/278kJ; Protein 1g; Carbohydrate 14.6g, of which sugars 14.5g; Fat 0.8g, of which saturates 0.1g; Cholesterol 0mg; Calcium 26mg; Fibre 2.9g; Sodium 7mg

Fruit Platter with Spices

A simple fresh fruit platter sprinkled with spices makes a healthy dessert. It is low in fat and offers a range of essential vitamins and minerals that are needed for good health.

Serves 6
1 pineapple
2 papayas
1 small melon
juice of 2 limes
2 pomegranates
ground ginger and ground nutmeg, for sprinkling
mint sprigs, to decorate

1 Peel the pineapple. Remove the core and any remaining eyes, then cut the flesh lengthwise into thin wedges.

2 Peel the papayas, cut them in half, scoop out the seeds, then cut into thin wedges.

3 Halve the melon and remove the seeds. Cut into thin wedges and remove the skin.

4 Arrange the fruit on six individual plates and sprinkle with the lime juice.

5 Cut the pomegranates in half using a sharp knife, then scoop out the seeds, discarding any pith.

6 Sprinkle the seeds over the fruit on the plates, then sprinkle the salad with a little ginger and nutmeg to taste.

7 Decorate with sprigs of fresh mint and serve immediately.

Cook's Tip
Also known as pawpaw, papaya are pear-shaped fruits from South America. When ripe, the green skin turns a speckled yellow and the pulp is a glorious orange/pink colour. The numerous edible, small black seeds taste peppery when dried. Peel off the skin using a sharp knife or vegetable peeler.

Figs & Pears in Honey

A stunningly simple dessert using fresh figs and pears scented with the warm fragrances of cinnamon and cardamom and drenched in a lemon and honey syrup.

Serves 4
1 lemon
90ml/6 tbsp clear honey
1 cinnamon stick
1 cardamom pod
350ml/12fl oz/1½ cups water
2 pears
8 fresh figs, halved

1 Pare the rind from the lemon using a cannelle knife (zester). Alternatively, use a vegetable peeler to remove the rind. Cut the pared rind into very thin strips.

2 Place the lemon rind, honey, cinnamon stick, cardamom pod and the water in a heavy pan and boil, uncovered, for about 10 minutes until reduced by about half.

3 Cut the pears into eighths, discarding the cores. Place in the syrup, add the figs and simmer for about 5 minutes, or until the fruit is tender.

4 Transfer the fruit to a serving bowl. Continue cooking the liquid until syrupy, then discard the cinnamon stick and cardamom pod and pour over the figs and pears to serve.

Cook's Tips
- *Leave the skin on the pears or discard, depending on your preference. The pears should not be too ripe otherwise they will disintegrate. Choose a type with a firm texture.*
- *Figs vary in colour from pale green and yellow to dark purple. When buying, look for firm fruit without any bruises or blemishes. A ripe fig will yield gently in your hand without having to press it.*
- *It is best to use pale green or light beige cardamom pods, rather than the coarser dark brown ones. Crush the cardamom with a rolling pin to split the pod slightly.*

Fruit platter with spices: Energy 55Kcal/229kJ; Protein 1g; Carbohydrate 12.9g, of which sugars 12.9g Fat 0.3g, of which saturates 0g; Cholesterol 0g; Fibre 2.3g; Calcium 25mg; Sodium 0g
Figs & pears in honey: Energy 143kcal/606kJ; Protein 1.7g; Carbohydrate 34.4g, of which sugars 34.4g; Fat 0.7g, of which saturates 0g; Cholesterol 0mg; Calcium 109mg; Fibre 4.7g; Sodium 28mg

Fruit Salad in Orange & Lemon Juice

A really good fruit salad is always popular, and this Italian dessert is certainly a winner. The fruit is bathed in fresh orange and lemon juices to produce a truly refreshing salad.

Serves 4–6

juice of 3 large sweet oranges
juice of 1 lemon
1 banana
1–2 apples
1 ripe pear
2 peaches or nectarines
4–5 apricots or plums
⅔ cup black or green grapes
⅔ cup berries (summer and/or winter)
any other fruits in season
sugar, to taste (optional)
2–3 tbsp Kirsch, maraschino or other liqueur (optional)

1 Place the freshly squeezed orange and lemon juices in a large serving bowl.

2 Wash or peel the fruits as necessary. Cut them all into bitesize pieces. Halve the grapes and remove the seeds if they have them. Core and slice the apples. Pit and slice soft fruits and leave small berries whole.

3 As soon as each fruit is prepared, add it to the bowl with the juices.

4 Taste the salad and add sugar to taste. Stir in the liqueur, if using.

5 Cover the bowl and chill for at least 2 hours. Mix well before serving.

Cook's Tip
Red, purple and black berries are the epitome of summer and autumn, though they are now likely to be available all year round. Try strawberries, raspberries, blueberries or blackberries.

Fruits-of-the-Tropics Salad

This is a creamy, exotic fruit salad flavoured with coconut milk and tasty nutmeg and cinnamon.

Serves 4–6

1 pineapple
400g/14oz can guava halves in syrup
2 bananas, sliced
1 large mango, peeled, stoned (pitted) and diced
115g/4oz stem ginger and 30ml/2 tbsp of the syrup
60ml/4 tbsp thick coconut milk
10ml/2 tsp sugar
2.5ml/½ tsp freshly grated nutmeg
2.5ml/½ tsp ground cinnamon
strips of coconut, to decorate

1 Peel, core and cube the pineapple, then place in a serving bowl.

2 Drain the guavas, reserving the syrup, and chop. Add the guavas to the bowl with one of the bananas and the mango.

3 Chop the stem ginger and add to the pineapple mixture.

4 Pour the 30 ml/2 tbsp of the ginger syrup and the reserved guava syrup into a blender or food processor and add the remaining banana, the coconut milk and the sugar. Blend to make a smooth, creamy purée.

5 Pour the banana and coconut purée over the fruit and add a little grated nutmeg and a sprinkling of cinnamon on top. Serve chilled, decorated with strips of coconut.

Cook's Tip
To dice mango, slice off a piece of flesh on either side of the stone (pit). Cut a cross-hatch pattern in the flesh of the slices, bend back the skin and scrape off the diced flesh.

Variation
Add a sliced kiwi fruit or seeded papaya for extra colour.

Fruit salad in orange & lemon juice: Energy 69kcal/295kJ; Protein 1g; Carbohydrate 17g, of which sugars 16.7g; Fat 0.2g, of which saturates 0g; Cholesterol 0mg; Calcium 15mg; Fibre 1.9g; Sodium 7mg
Fruits-of-the-tropics salad: Energy 165kcal/706kJ; Protein 1.5g; Carbohydrate 41.4g, of which sugars 40.5g; Fat 0.5g, of which saturates 0.1g; Cholesterol 0mg; Calcium 46mg; Fibre 4.8g; Sodium 41mg

Exotic Fruit Salad in Pineapple Cases

A mix of exotic fruit served up in attractive pineapple cases makes an impressive dinner party dessert.

Serves 4

75g/3oz/scant ½ cup sugar
300ml/½ pint/1¼ cups water
30ml/2 tbsp stem ginger syrup
2 pieces star anise
2.5cm/1in cinnamon stick
1 clove
juice of ½ lemon
2 fresh mint sprigs
1 mango
2 bananas, sliced
8 lychees, fresh or canned
225g/8oz/2 cups strawberries
2 pieces stem ginger, cut into sticks
1 pineapple

1 Place the sugar in a pan and add the water, ginger syrup, spices, lemon juice and mint. Bring to the boil and simmer for 3 minutes. Strain into a large bowl.

2 Remove both the top and bottom from the mango and remove the outer skin. Stand the mango on one end and remove the flesh in two pieces either side of the flat stone. Slice evenly and add to the syrup. Add the bananas, lychees, strawberries and ginger. Chill until ready to serve.

3 Cut the pineapple in half down the centre. Loosen the flesh with a small, serrated knife and remove to form two boat shapes. Cut the pineapple flesh into large chunks and place in the cooled syrup.

4 Spoon the fruit salad carefully into the pineapple halves and bring to the table on a large serving dish or board. There will be enough fruit salad left over to be able to offer refills for second helpings.

Variation
A variety of fruits can be used for this salad. Look out for fresh mandarin oranges, star fruit, papaya, physalis and passion fruit.

Cool Green Fruit Salad

A stylish yet simple fruit salad for any time of the year. Serve with amaretti or crisp almond cookies.

Serves 6

3 Ogen or Galia melons
115g/4oz seedless green grapes
2 kiwi fruit
1 star fruit
1 green-skinned apple
1 lime
175ml/6fl oz/¾ cup sparkling grape juice

1 Cut the melons in half and remove the seeds. Keeping the shells intact, scoop out the flesh with a melon baller, or scoop it out with a spoon and cut into bitesize cubes. Reserve the melon shells.

2 Remove any stems from the grapes and, if they are large, cut them in half. Peel and chop the kiwi fruit. Thinly slice the star fruit. Core and thinly slice the apple. Place the grapes, kiwi fruit and apple in a mixing bowl with the melon.

3 Thinly pare the rind from the lime and cut it in fine strips. Blanch the lime strips in boiling water for 30 seconds, drain and rinse in cold water. Reserve for garnishing.

4 Squeeze the juice from the lime and toss the juice into the bowl of fruit.

5 Spoon the prepared fruit into the reserved melon shells and chill the shells until required.

6 Just before serving, spoon the sparkling grape juice over the fruit and scatter with the strips of lime rind.

Cook's Tip
On a hot summer's day, serve the filled melon shells nestling on a platter of crushed ice to keep them beautifully cool.

Pineapple fruit salad: Energy 82kcal/348kJ; Protein 1.2g; Carbohydrate 18.3g, of which sugars 18.1g; Fat 1g, of which saturates 0.1g; Cholesterol 0mg; Calcium 33mg; Fibre 3.7g; Sodium 9mg
Cool green fruit salad: Energy 102kcal/436kJ; Protein 1.7g; Carbohydrate 24.4g, of which sugars 24.4g; Fat 0.4g, of which saturates 0g; Cholesterol 0mg; Calcium 46mg; Fibre 1.9g; Sodium 81mg

Fresh Fig, Apple & Date Salad

Sweet Mediterranean figs and dates combine especially well with crisp dessert apples in this unusual fruit salad.

Serves 4

6 large apples
juice of ½ lemon
175g/6oz/generous 1 cup fresh dates
25g/1oz white marzipan
5ml/1 tsp orange flower water
60ml/4 tbsp natural (plain) yogurt
4 ripe green or purple figs
4 almonds, toasted

1 Core the apples. Slice thinly, then cut into fine matchsticks. Moisten with lemon juice to keep them white.

2 Remove the stones from the dates and cut the flesh into fine strips, then combine them with the apple slices.

3 Soften the marzipan with the orange flower water and combine with the yogurt. Mix well.

4 Pile the prepared apples and dates in the centre of four individual serving plates.

5 Remove the stem from each of the figs and divide the fruit into quarters without cutting right through the base. Squeeze the base with the thumb and forefinger of each hand to open up the fig.

6 Place a fig in the centre of each fruit salad, spoon in the yogurt filling and decorate with a toasted almond.

Cook's Tip

Choose unbruised, ripe figs that yield to gentle pressure and eat them on the day of purchase. If they are not too ripe they can be kept in the fridge for a day or two.

Fruit with Yogurt & Honey

Fresh fruit most commonly follows a meal in Greece, and the addition of yogurt and honey makes it even more delicious.

Serves 4

225g/8oz/1 cup Greek (US strained plain) yogurt
45ml/3 tbsp clear honey
selection of fresh fruit for dipping, such as apples, pears, tangerines, grapes, figs and strawberries

1 Beat the yogurt, place in a dish, and stir in the honey, to leave a marbled effect.

2 Cut the fruits into wedges or bitesize pieces, or leave whole.

3 Arrange the fruits on a platter with the bowl of dip in the centre. Serve chilled.

Figs with Honey & Wine

Cooled poached figs make a salad with a difference. They are delicious served with sweetened whipped cream flavoured with vanilla extract.

Serves 6

450ml/¾ pint/scant 2 cups dry white wine
75g/3oz/⅓ cup clear honey
50g/2oz/¼ cup caster (superfine) sugar
1 small orange
8 whole cloves
450g/1lb fresh figs
1 cinnamon stick

1 Put the wine, honey and sugar in a heavy pan and heat gently until the sugar dissolves.

2 Stud the orange with the cloves and add to the syrup with the figs and cinnamon. Cover and simmer gently for 5–10 minutes until the figs are softened. Transfer to a serving dish and leave to cool completely before serving.

Fresh fig, apple & date salad: Energy 223kcal/943kJ; Protein 4.5g; Carbohydrate 43.8g, of which sugars 43.7g; Fat 4.5g, of which saturates 0.4g; Cholesterol 0mg; Calcium 170mg; Fibre 4.8g; Sodium 46mg
Fruit with yogurt & honey: Energy 131kcal/548kJ; Protein 4.7g; Carbohydrate 17.2g, of which sugars 17.2g; Fat 5.9g, of which saturates 2.9g; Cholesterol 0mg; Calcium 105mg; Fibre 1.4g; Sodium 49mg
Figs with honey & wine: Energy 316kcal/1318kJ; Protein 1.8g; Carbohydrate 29.7g, of which sugars 29.7g; Fat 18.4g, of which saturates 11.1g; Cholesterol 46mg; Calcium 101mg; Fibre 2.3g; Sodium 30mg

Pineapple, Strawberries & Lychees

The sweet, tropical flavours of pineapple and lychees combine well with richly scented strawberries to create a most refreshing salad. The pineapple shells make lovely bowls.

Serves 4

2 small pineapples
450g/1lb/4 cups strawberries
400g/14oz can lychees
45ml/3 tbsp kirsch or white rum
30ml/2 tbsp icing (confectioners') sugar

1 Remove the crowns from both pineapples by twisting sharply. Reserve the leaves for decoration.

2 Cut both pineapples in half diagonally using a large, serrated knife. Cut around the flesh inside the skin of both pineapples with a small, serrated knife, keeping the skin intact. Remove the core from the pineapple and discard.

3 Chop the pineapple flesh and put in a freezerproof bowl. Reserve the skins.

4 Hull the strawberries and gently combine with the pineapple and lychees, taking care not to damage the fruit.

5 Mix the kirsch or rum with the icing sugar, pour over the fruit and freeze for 45 minutes.

6 Turn out the fruit into the pineapple skin shells, decorate with the reserved pineapple leaves and serve.

Cook's Tips

- *A ripe pineapple will resist pressure when squeezed and will have a sweet, fragrant smell. In winter freezing conditions can cause the flesh to blacken.*
- *Make sure you remove all the brown 'eyes' from the pineapple before cutting into pieces.*
- *The pineapple can be chopped finely to create almost a 'crush' which will coat the other fruit.*

Winter Fruit Salad

This colourful dessert is guaranteed to brighten up the winter months. It tastes luscious served with thick yogurt or cream.

Serves 6

225g/8oz can pineapple cubes in fruit juice
200ml/7fl oz/scant 1 cup freshly squeezed orange juice
200ml/7fl oz/scant 1 cup unsweetened apple juice
30ml/2 tbsp orange or apple liqueur
30ml/2 tbsp clear honey (optional)
2 oranges
2 green apples
2 pears
4 plums, stoned (pitted) and chopped
12 fresh dates, stoned (pitted) and chopped
115g/4oz/½ cup ready-to-eat dried apricots
fresh mint sprigs, to decorate

1 Drain the pineapple, reserving the juice. Put the pineapple juice, orange juice, apple juice, liqueur and honey, if using, in a large serving bowl and stir.

2 To segment the oranges, cut a slice off the top and bottom of each orange to expose the flesh. Place on a board and remove the skin, cutting downwards. Take care to remove all the white pith. Cut between the membranes to release the segments.

3 Put the orange and pineapple in the fruit juice mixture.

4 Peel, core and slice the apples and pears and add to the serving bowl.

5 Stir in the chopped plums, dates and dried apricots to combine well. Cover and chill for several hours.

6 Decorate with fresh mint sprigs to serve.

Variation

Use other unsweetened fruit juices such as pink grapefruit and pineapple juice in place of the orange and apple juice.

Pineapple, strawberries & lychees: Energy 235kcal/999kJ; Protein 2.2g; Carbohydrate 52.5g, of which sugars 52.5g; Fat 0.5g, of which saturates 0g; Cholesterol 0mg; Calcium 62mg; Fibre 4.2g; Sodium 13mg
Winter fruit salad: Energy 141kcal/603kJ; Protein 1.9g; Carbohydrate 32g, of which sugars 32g; Fat 0.4g, of which saturates 0g; Cholesterol 0mg; Calcium 60mg; Fibre 4.2g; Sodium 12mg

Citrus Fruit Flambé

A fruit flambé makes a dramatic finale for a dinner party. Topping this refreshing citrus salad with praline makes it extra special.

Serves 4

4 oranges
2 ruby grapefruit
2 limes
50g/2oz/¼ cup butter
50g/2oz/¼ cup muscovado (molasses) sugar
45ml/3 tbsp Cointreau
fresh mint sprigs, to decorate

For the praline

oil, for greasing
115g/4oz/½ cup caster (superfine) sugar
50g/2oz/¼ cup pistachio nuts

1 First, make the praline. Brush a baking sheet lightly with oil. Place the caster sugar and nuts in a small, heavy-based saucepan and cook gently, swirling the pan occasionally until the sugar has melted.

2 Continue to cook over a fairly low heat until the nuts start to pop and the sugar has turned a dark golden colour. Pour on to the oiled baking sheet and set aside to cool.

3 Using a sharp knife, chop the praline into rough chunks.

4 Cut all the rind and pith from the citrus fruit. Holding each fruit in turn over a large bowl, cut between the membranes so that the segments fall into the bowl, with any juice.

5 Heat the butter and muscovado sugar together in a heavy-based frying pan until the sugar has melted and the mixture is golden. Strain the citrus juices into the pan and continue to cook, stirring occasionally, until the juice has reduced and is syrupy.

6 Add the fruit segments and warm through without stirring.

7 Pour over the Cointreau and set it alight. As soon as the flames die down, spoon the fruit flambé into serving dishes. Scatter some praline over each portion and decorate with mint.

Oranges with Caramel Wigs

The slightly bitter, caramelized orange rind and syrup has a wonderful flavour and texture that sits in perfect contrast to the sweet, juicy oranges.

Serves 6

6 oranges
120g/4oz/generous ½ cup caster (superfine) sugar
120ml/4fl oz/½ cup boiling water

1 Using a cannelle knife (zester) or vegetable peeler, pare the rind of a few of the oranges to make 12 long strips. Set aside.

2 Using a sharp knife, peel all the oranges, discarding the pith and reserving the juice that collects. Freeze the oranges separately for 30 minutes.

3 Slice the oranges evenly, then pile up the slices to reform their shape. Secure the recreated oranges with a cocktail stick (toothpick). Chill.

4 To make the wigs, simmer the 12 rind strips for about 5 minutes, then drain, rinse, and repeat. Trim with scissors.

5 Put half the sugar into a small pan and add 15ml/1 tbsp water. Heat gently until the mixture caramelizes, shaking the pan a little if one side starts to brown too fast. As soon as the mixture colours, dip the bottom of the pan into cold water. Add 30ml/2 tbsp hot water and the orange rind to the caramel, then stir until the caramel dissolves. Turn the rind onto a plate to cool.

6 To make a caramel syrup for serving, put the remaining sugar in a small pan with 15ml/1 tbsp water, and make caramel as in the previous step. When it has coloured nicely, stand well back, pour in the boiling water and stir with a wooden spoon to dissolve. Add the reserved orange juices and pour into a serving jug (pitcher).

7 To serve, arrange the orange strips in a criss-cross pattern on top of each orange. Remove the cocktail sticks and pour a little caramel syrup round the base of each orange.

Citrus fruit flambé: Energy 446kcal/1872kJ; Protein 4.8g; Carbohydrate 65.2g, of which sugars 64.8g; Fat 17.4g, of which saturates 7.4g; Cholesterol 27mg; Calcium 127mg; Fibre 4.4g; Sodium 155mg
Oranges with caramel wigs: Energy 122kcal/521kJ; Protein 1.4g; Carbohydrate 30.8g, of which sugars 30.8g; Fat 0.1g, of which saturates 0g; Cholesterol 0mg; Calcium 66mg; Fibre 2g; Sodium 7mg

Pistachio & Rose Water Oranges

This light and tangy dessert is perfect to serve after a heavy main course, such as a hearty meat stew or a leg of roast lamb. Combining three favourite Middle-Eastern ingredients, it is delightfully fragrant and refreshing. If you don't have pistachio nuts, use hazelnuts instead.

Serves 4

4 large oranges
30ml/2 tbsp rose water
30ml/2 tbsp shelled pistachio nuts, roughly chopped

1 Slice the top and bottom off one of the oranges to expose the flesh. Using a small serrated knife, slice down between the pith and the flesh, working round the orange, to remove all the peel and pith. Slice the orange into six rounds, reserving any juice. Repeat with the remaining oranges.

2 Arrange the oranges in a shallow dish. Mix the reserved juice with the rose water and drizzle over the oranges.

3 Cover the dish with clear film (plastic wrap) and chill for about 30 minutes. Sprinkle the chopped pistachio nuts over the oranges and serve immediately.

Cook's Tips

- *Rose-scented sugar is delicious sprinkled over fresh fruit salads. Wash and thoroughly dry a handful of rose petals and place in a sealed container filled with caster (superfine) sugar for 2–3 days. Remove the petals before using the sugar.*
- *This salad is delicious served with vanilla cream. Put 150ml/¼ pint/⅔ cup double (heavy) cream in a small pan with a vanilla pod (bean). Bring almost to the boil, then leave to cool and steep for 30 minutes. Remove the vanilla pod, then transfer the cream to a bowl. Mix with another 150ml/¼ pint/⅔ cup cream and caster (superfine) sugar to taste. Whip lightly.*

Clementines with Star Anise

A perfect choice for the festive season, this fresh-tasting salad is delicately flavoured with mulling spices. Serve with whipped cream and sweet finger biscuits for a lovely dessert to follow a traditional turkey dish.

Serves 6

rind of 1 lime
350ml/12fl oz/1½ cups sweet dessert wine, such as Sauternes
75g/3oz/6 tbsp caster (superfine) sugar
6 star anise
1 cinnamon stick
1 vanilla pod (bean)
30ml/2 tbsp Cointreau or other orange liqueur
12 clementines

1 Using a cannelle knife (zester) or vegetable peeler, thinly pare two strips of rind from the lime. Put in a pan, together with the wine, sugar, star anise and cinnamon.

2 Split the vanilla pod and add it to the pan. Bring to the boil, then lower the heat and simmer for 10 minutes.

3 Remove the pan from the heat and leave to cool, then stir in the orange-flavoured liqueur.

4 Peel the clementines. Cut some of them in half and place them all in a dish.

5 Pour the wine mixture over the clementines and chill before serving.

Cook's Tips

- *Clementines are small, sweet and easy to peel.*
- *They are most predominantly available throughout the winter months.*
- *Select clementines that are firm and heavy for their size and make sure they don't have soft spots or wrinkled skin.*

Pistachio & rose water oranges: Energy 101kcal/424kJ; Protein 3g; Carbohydrate 13.4g, of which sugars 13.2g; Fat 4.3g, of which saturates 0.6g; Cholesterol 0mg; Calcium 79mg; Fibre 3g; Sodium 47mg
Clementines with star anise: Energy 149kcal/632kJ; Protein 0.9g; Carbohydrate 24.7g, of which sugars 24.7g; Fat 0.1g, of which saturates 0g; Cholesterol 0mg; Calcium 40mg; Fibre 1g; Sodium 12mg

Jamaican Fruit Trifle

This trifle is actually based on a Caribbean fool that consists of fruit stirred into thick vanilla-flavoured cream. This is a lighter version of the original.

Serves 8

1 large sweet pineapple, peeled and cored, about 350g/12oz
300ml/½pint/1¼ cups double (heavy) cream
200ml/7fl oz/scant 1 cup crème fraîche
60ml/4 tbsp icing (confectioners') sugar, sifted
10ml/2 tsp pure vanilla extract
30ml/2 tbsp white or coconut rum
3 papayas, peeled, seeded and chopped
3 mangoes, peeled, stoned (pitted) and chopped
thinly pared rind and juice of 1 lime
25g/1oz/⅓ cup coarsely shredded or flaked coconut, toasted

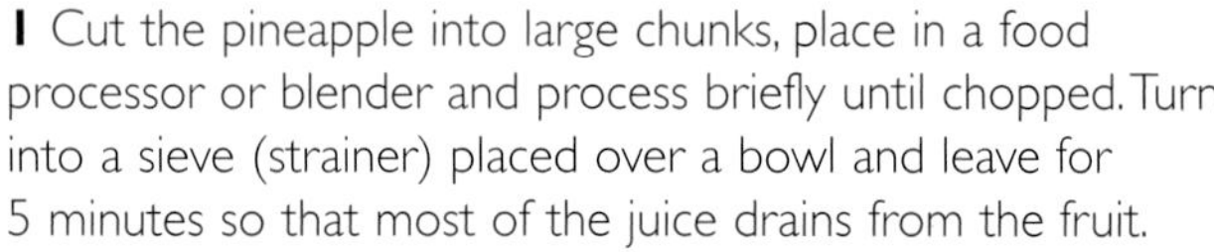

1 Cut the pineapple into large chunks, place in a food processor or blender and process briefly until chopped. Turn into a sieve (strainer) placed over a bowl and leave for 5 minutes so that most of the juice drains from the fruit.

2 Whip the double cream to very soft peaks, then lightly but thoroughly fold in the crème fraîche, sifted icing sugar, vanilla extract and rum. Fold in the drained pineapple.

3 Place the papaya and mango in a large bowl and pour over the lime juice. Gently stir to mix. Shred the pared lime rind.

4 Divide the fruit mixture and the pineapple cream between eight dessert plates. Decorate with the lime shreds, toasted coconut and a few small pineapple leaves, if you like.

Cook's Tip
It is important to let the pineapple purée drain thoroughly, otherwise the pineapple cream will be watery. Don't throw away the drained pineapple juice – mix it with fizzy mineral water for a refreshing drink.

Zingy Fruit Salad of Papaya, Lime & Ginger

This refreshing, fruity salad makes a lovely light breakfast, perfect for the summer months. Choose really ripe and fragrant papayas for the best flavour.

Serves 4

2 large ripe papayas
juice of 1 fresh lime
2 pieces preserved stem ginger, finely sliced

1 Cut the papaya in half lengthwise and scoop out the seeds, using a teaspoon.

2 Using a sharp knife, cut the flesh into thin slices and arrange on a platter.

3 Squeeze the lime juice over the papaya and sprinkle with the sliced stem ginger. Serve immediately.

Cook's Tips
- *Papayas are also known as pawpaws.*
- *Ripe papayas have a yellowish speckled skin and feel soft to the touch. Their orange-coloured flesh has an attractive, smooth texture.*
- *Ripe papayas have a perfumed aroma and sweet flavour, which makes them perfect for eating raw.*
- *To ripen an unripe fruit, place it in a paper bag with an already ripened fruit, and leave at room temperature or in a warm place.*

Variation
This refreshing fruit salad is delicious made with many other tropical fruits. Try using two ripe peeled mangoes instead of the papayas.

Jamaican fruit trifle: Energy 479kcal/1995kJ; Protein 2.3g; Carbohydrate 41g, of which sugars 40.7g; Fat 34.2g, of which saturates 22.7g; Cholesterol 80mg; Calcium 79mg; Fibre 3.6g; Sodium 27mg
Zingy papaya, lime & ginger salad: Energy 55kcal/233kJ; Protein 0.8g; Carbohydrate 13.4g, of which sugars 13.4g; Fat 0.2g, of which saturates 0g; Cholesterol 0mg; Calcium 35mg; Fibre 3.3g; Sodium 8mg

Minted Pomegranate Yogurt with Grapefruit Salad

The flavourful yogurt is delicious for breakfast, but also makes a fabulous dessert when served with a delicately scented citrus fruit salad.

Serves 3–4

300ml/½ pint/1¼ cups Greek (US strained plain) yogurt
2–3 ripe pomegranates
1 small bunch mint, finely chopped
honey or sugar, to taste (optional)
handful of pomegranate seeds and mint leaves, to decorate

For the grapefruit salad
2 red grapefruits
2 pink grapefruits
1 white grapefruit
15–30ml/1–2 tbsp orange flower water

1 Put the yogurt in a bowl and beat well. Cut open the pomegranates and scoop out the seeds, removing all the pith.

2 Fold the pomegranate seeds and chopped mint into the yogurt. Sweeten with a little honey or sugar, if using, then chill.

3 Remove the peel from the grapefruits, cutting off all the pith. Cut between the membranes to remove the segments, holding the fruit over a bowl to catch the juices. Discard the membranes. Mix the fruit segments with the reserved juices.

4 Sprinkle the grapefruit segments with the orange flower water and add a little honey or sugar, if using. Stir gently then decorate with a few pomegranate seeds.

5 Decorate the chilled yogurt with a scattering of pomegranate seeds and mint leaves, and serve with the grapefruit salad.

Variation
Alternatively, you can use a mixture of oranges and blood oranges, interspersed with thin segments of lemon.

Jungle Fruits in Lemon Grass Syrup

A luscious mix of exotic fruit, bathed in a delicious syrup flavoured with lemon grass, this salad would make a perfect finish to an Oriental-style meal.

Serves 6

1 firm papaya
1 small pineapple
2 small star fruit, sliced into stars
1 can preserved lychees or 12 fresh lychees, peeled and stoned (pitted)
2 firm yellow or green bananas, peeled and cut diagonally into slices

For the syrup
225ml/7½fl oz/1 cup water
115g/4oz/generous ½ cup caster (superfine) sugar
2 lemon grass stalks, bruised

1 To make the syrup, put the water into a heavy pan with the sugar and bruised lemon grass stalks. Bring the liquid to the boil, stirring constantly until the sugar has dissolved, then reduce the heat and simmer for 10–15 minutes. Leave to cool.

2 Peel and halve the papaya, remove the seeds and slice the flesh crossways.

3 Peel the pineapple and slice it into rounds. Remove the core and cut each round in half.

4 Put all the fruit into a bowl. Pour the syrup, including the lemon grass stalks, over the top and toss lightly to combine.

5 Cover and chill for at least 6 hours, or overnight, to allow the flavours to mingle. Remove the lemon grass stalks before serving.

Variations
This fruit salad can be made with any combination of tropical fruits – just go for a good balance of colour, flavour and texture. To give the salad a softly spiced flavour, try flavouring the syrup with a little finely chopped, peeled fresh root ginger rather than lemon grass.

Yogurt with salad: Energy 188kcal/784kJ; Protein 8.8g; Carbohydrate 18g, of which sugars 18g; Fat 10.5g, of which saturates 5.2g; Cholesterol 0mg; Calcium 202mg; Fibre 3.6g; Sodium 82mg
Jungle fruits in lemon grass syrup: Energy 174kcal/742kJ; Protein 1.3g; Carbohydrate 44.2g, of which sugars 43.4g; Fat 0.3g, of which saturates 0g; Cholesterol 0mg; Calcium 38mg; Fibre 2.7g; Sodium 6mg

Watermelon, Ginger & Pink Grapefruit Salad

A pretty, pink salad with the slightly tart grapefruit contrasting nicely with the sweet ginger.

Serves 4
450g/1lb/2 cups watermelon flesh
2 ruby or pink grapefruit
2 pieces stem ginger and 30ml/2 tbsp of the syrup

1 Remove any seeds from the watermelon and cut the flesh into bitesize chunks.

2 Using a small, sharp knife, cut away all the peel and white pith from the pink grapefruit.

3 Carefully remove the segments from between the membranes, catching any juice in a bowl.

4 Finely chop the stem ginger and place in a serving bowl with the cubes of melon and grapefruit segments, adding the reserved grapefruit juice.

5 Spoon over the ginger syrup. Toss the fruits lightly to mix. Chill before serving.

Cook's Tips
- *Look for watermelons that feel heavy for their size and yield to gentle pressure at the stem end.*
- *Grapefruit flesh ranges in colour from vivid pink and ruby red to white; the pink and red varieties are sweeter. Heavier fruits are likely to be juicier.*
- *Stem ginger is also known as preserved ginger and is available in most supermarkets. It is young ginger, preserved in sugar syrup. Its sweetness provides contrast to the grapefruit.*
- *Toss the fruits gently – grapefruit segments break up easily and can make the salad look unattractive.*

Grapefruit Salad with Campari & Orange

The bitter-sweet flavour of Campari combines especially well with the citrus fruit to produce a refreshing salad for any time of the year.

Serves 4
150ml/¼ pint/⅔ cup water
45 ml/3 tbsp caster (superfine) sugar
60ml/4 tbsp Campari
30ml/2 tbsp lemon juice
4 grapefruit
5 oranges
4 fresh mint sprigs, to decorate

1 Bring the water to the boil in a small pan, add the sugar and simmer until dissolved. Transfer to a bowl, allow to cool, then add the Campari and lemon juice. Chill until ready to serve.

2 Slice the top and bottom off one of the grapefruit to expose the flesh. Using a small serrated knife, slice down between the pith and the flesh, working round the grapefruit, to remove all the peel and pith.

3 Release the segments by cutting between the flesh and the membranes, working over a bowl to catch the juices. Repeat with the remaining grapefruit and the oranges.

4 Add the grapefruit and orange segments to the bowl of Campari syrup and chill.

5 Spoon the salad into four dishes, decorate each with a sprig of fresh mint and serve.

Cook's Tips
- *When buying citrus fruit, choose brightly-coloured varieties that feel heavy for their size.*
- *Before you discard the citrus fruit membranes, squeeze as much juice as possible from them into the bowl of juice.*

Watermelon, ginger & grapefruit salad: Energy 85kcal/362kJ; Protein 1.3g; Carbohydrate 20.3g, of which sugars 20.3g; Fat 0.5g, of which saturates 0.1g; Cholesterol 0mg; Calcium 28mg; Fibre 1.2g; Sodium 25mg
Grapefruit salad: Energy 181kcal/766kJ; Protein 3g; Carbohydrate 35.4g, of which sugars 35.4g; Fat 0.3g, of which saturates 0g; Cholesterol 0mg; Calcium 113mg; Fibre 4.6g; Sodium 13mg

Fruit Kebabs with Mango & Yogurt Sauce

Enjoy these mixed fruit kebabs dipped into a refreshingly minty mango and yogurt sauce.

Serves 4

½ pineapple, peeled, cored and cubed
2 kiwi fruit, peeled and cubed
150g/5oz/scant 1 cup strawberries, hulled and cut in half lengthwise if large
½ mango, peeled, stoned (pitted) and cubed

For the sauce

120ml/4fl oz/½ cup fresh mango purée, made from 1–1½ peeled and stoned (pitted) mangoes
120ml/4fl oz/½ cup thick natural (plain) yogurt
5ml/1 tsp sugar
few drops of vanilla extract
15ml/1 tbsp finely shredded fresh mint leaves
1 fresh mint sprig, to decorate

1 To make the sauce, beat together the mango purée, yogurt, sugar and vanilla with an electric hand mixer.

2 Stir in the shredded mint. Cover the sauce and chill until required.

3 Thread the fruit on to twelve 15cm/6in wooden skewers, alternating the pineapple, kiwi fruit, strawberries and mango.

4 Transfer the mango and yogurt sauce to an attractive bowl, decorate with a mint sprig and place in the centre of a large serving platter. Surround with the kebabs and serve.

Variations

- *Instead of flavouring the sauce with vanilla extract, add some finely chopped preserved stem ginger with a little of the syrup from the jar.*
- *For a pink sauce, replace the mango purée with strawberry or raspberry purée, sweetened with icing (confectioners') sugar.*

Papaya, Mango and Star Fruit in Cinnamon Syrup

These glistening fruits, bathed in a delicately-flavoured syrup, provide an attractive way to round off a meal. The salad is particularly good served with mango or vanilla ice cream, or thick yogurt.

Serves 6

450g/1lb/2¼ cups caster (superfine) sugar
1 cinnamon stick
1 large or 2 medium papayas (about 675g/1½lb), peeled, seeded and cut lengthwise into thin pieces
1 large or 2 medium mangoes (about 675g/1½lb) peeled, stoned (pitted) and cut lengthwise into thin pieces
1 large or 2 small star fruit (about 225g/8oz) thinly sliced

1 Sprinkle one-third of the sugar over the bottom of a large pan. Add the cinnamon stick and half of the papaya, mango and star fruit pieces.

2 Sprinkle half of the remaining sugar over the fruit pieces in the pan. Add the rest of the fruit and sugar.

3 Cover the pan and cook the fruit over medium heat for 35–45 minutes, until the sugar dissolves completely. Shake the pan occasionally, but do not stir or the fruit will collapse.

4 Uncover the pan and simmer for about 10 minutes, until the fruit begins to appear translucent, then remove the pan from the heat and allow to cool. Discard the cinnamon stick.

5 Transfer the fruit and syrup to a bowl, cover and refrigerate overnight before serving.

Cook's Tip
This salad is best prepared a day in advance to allow the flavours to develop properly.

Fruit kebabs with mango & yogurt sauce: Energy 120kcal/513kJ; Protein 3g; Carbohydrate 27.1g, of which sugars 26.9g; Fat 0.8g, of which saturates 0.2g; Cholesterol 0mg; Calcium 97mg; Fibre 3.7g; Sodium 32mg
Tropical fruits in cinnamon syrup: Energy 413kcal/1765kJ; Protein 1.8g; Carbohydrate 107.5g, of which sugars 107.1g; Fat 0.4g, of which saturates 0.1g; Cholesterol 0mg; Calcium 81mg; Fibre 6g; Sodium 13mg

Blackberry Salad with Rose Granita

In this elegant dessert, a rose-flavoured granita is served over strips of white meringue and set off by a blackberry salad.

Serves 4

150g/5oz/⅔ cup caster (superfine) sugar
1 fresh red rose, petals finely chopped
5ml/1 tsp rose water
10ml/2 tsp lemon juice
450g/1lb/2⅔ cups blackberries
icing (confectioners') sugar, for dusting
fresh rose petals, to decorate

For the meringue

2 egg whites
115g/4oz/generous ½ cup caster (superfine) sugar

1 To make the granita, bring 150ml/¼ pint/⅔ cup water to the boil in a stainless-steel or enamel pan. Add the sugar and rose petals, then simmer for 5 minutes.

2 Strain the syrup into a deep metal tray, add a further 450 ml/¾ pint/scant 2 cups water, the rose water and lemon juice and leave to cool. Freeze for 3 hours, or until solid.

3 Meanwhile, preheat the oven to 140°C/275°F/Gas 1. Line a baking sheet with six layers of newspaper and cover with non-stick baking parchment.

4 To make the meringue, whisk the egg whites until they hold their weight on the whisk. Add the caster sugar a little at a time, and whisk until firm.

5 Spoon the meringue into a piping bag fitted with a 1cm/½in plain nozzle. Pipe the meringue in lengths across the paper-lined baking sheet. Dry the meringue near the bottom of the oven for 1½–2 hours.

6 Break the meringue into 5cm/2in lengths and place three or four pieces on each of four large serving plates. Pile the blackberries next to the meringue. With a tablespoon, scrape the granita finely. Shape into ovals and place over the meringue. Dust with icing sugar, decorate with rose petals, and serve.

Blueberry & Orange Salad with Lavender Meringue

Delicate blueberries feature here in a simple salad of sharp oranges and sweet little meringues flavoured with fresh lavender.

Serves 4

6 oranges
350g/12oz/3 cups blueberries
8 fresh lavender sprigs, to decorate

For the meringue

2 egg whites
115g/4oz/generous ½ cup caster (superfine) sugar
5ml/1 tsp fresh lavender flowers

1 Preheat the oven to 140°C/275°F/Gas 1. Line a baking sheet with six layers of newspaper and cover with non-stick baking parchment.

2 To make the meringue, whisk the egg whites in a large mixing bowl until they hold their weight on the whisk. Add the sugar a little at a time, whisking thoroughly before each addition. Fold in the lavender flowers.

3 Spoon the lavender meringue into a piping bag fitted with a 5mm/¼in plain nozzle. Pipe as many small buttons of meringue onto the prepared baking sheet as you can. Dry the meringues near the bottom of the oven for 1½–2 hours.

4 To segment the oranges, remove the peel from the top, bottom and sides with a serrated knife. Loosen the segments by cutting with a paring knife between the flesh and the membranes, holding the fruit over a bowl.

5 Arrange the orange segments on four individual plates.

6 Combine the blueberries with the lavender meringues and pile in the centre of each plate. Decorate with sprigs of lavender and serve immediately.

Blackberry salad with rose granita: Energy 292kcal/1243kJ; Protein 2.1g; Carbohydrate 75g, of which sugars 75g; Fat 0.2g, of which saturates 0g; Cholesterol 0mg; Calcium 82mg; Fibre 3.5g; Sodium 22mg
Blueberry, orange & lavender salad: Energy 215kcal/915kJ; Protein 4.6g; Carbohydrate 51.5g, of which sugars 51.5g; Fat 0.4g, of which saturates 0g; Cholesterol 0mg; Calcium 146mg; Fibre 6.1g; Sodium 44mg

Raspberries with Mango Custard

This remarkable salad unites the sharp quality of fresh raspberries with a special custard made from rich, fragrant mangoes.

Serves 4
1 large mango
3 egg yolks
30ml/2 tbsp caster (superfine) sugar
10ml/2 tsp cornflour (cornstarch)
200ml/7fl oz/scant 1 cup milk
8 fresh mint sprigs, to decorate

For the raspberry sauce
450g/1lb/2⅔ cups raspberries
45ml/3 tbsp caster (superfine) sugar

1 To prepare the mango, remove the top and bottom with a serrated knife. Cut away the outer skin, then remove the flesh by cutting either side of the flat central stone. Save half of the mango flesh for decoration and roughly chop the remainder.

2 For the custard, combine the egg yolks, sugar, cornflour and 30ml/2 tbsp of the milk in a small bowl until smooth.

3 Rinse a small pan with cold water to prevent the milk from catching. Bring the rest of the milk to the boil in the pan, pour it over the ingredients in the bowl and stir evenly. Strain the mixture back into the pan, stir to simmering point and cook, stirring, until thickened.

4 Pour the custard into a food processor, add the chopped mango and blend until smooth. Allow the custard to cool.

5 To make the raspberry sauce, place 350g/12oz/2 cups of the raspberries in a stain-resistant pan. Add the sugar, soften over a gentle heat and simmer for 5 minutes. Rub the fruit through a fine nylon sieve (strainer) to remove the seeds. Allow to cool.

6 Spoon the raspberry sauce and mango custard into two pools on four individual plates. Slice the reserved mango and arrange over the raspberry sauce. Scatter the remaining raspberries over the mango custard. Decorate with mint.

Melon & Strawberry Salad

A beautiful and colourful fruit salad, this is equally suitable to serve as a refreshing appetizer or to round off a meal.

Serves 4
1 Galia melon
1 honeydew melon
½ watermelon
225g/8oz/2 cups strawberries
15ml/1 tbsp lemon juice
15ml/1 tbsp clear honey
15ml/1 tbsp chopped fresh mint
1 fresh mint sprig (optional)

1 To prepare the melons, cut them in half and discard the seeds. Use a melon baller to scoop out the flesh into balls. Alternatively, use a knife and cut the melon flesh into cubes. Place the melon in a fruit bowl.

2 Rinse and hull the strawberries, cut in half and add to the melon balls or cubes.

3 Mix together the lemon juice and honey and add about 15ml/1 tbsp water to make it easier to spoon over the fruit. Mix into the fruit gently.

4 Sprinkle the chopped mint over the top of the fruit. Serve the fruit salad decorated with the mint sprig, if wished.

Cook's Tip
Do not rinse the strawberries until just before serving, otherwise they will turn mushy. When buying in punnets, remember that a strong scent means a good flavour. Fruit in season is best.

Variation
Use whichever melons are available: replace Galia with cantaloupe or watermelon with Charentais, for example. Try to choose three melons with a variation in colour.

Raspberriess with mango custard: Energy 213kcal/903kJ; Protein 6.4g; Carbohydrate 34.7g, of which sugars 32.3g; Fat 6.5g, of which saturates 2.2g; Cholesterol 193mg; Calcium 125mg; Fibre 3.8g; Sodium 37mg
Melon & strawberry salad: Energy 204kcal/867kJ; Protein 3.9g; Carbohydrate 47.5g, of which sugars 47.5g; Fat 1.2g, of which saturates 0.3g; Cholesterol 0mg; Calcium 66mg; Fibre 2.9g; Sodium 128mg

Cantaloupe Melon with Grilled Strawberries

If strawberries are slightly underripe, sprinkling them with a little sugar and grilling them will help bring out their flavour.

Serves 4

115g/4oz/1 cup strawberries
15ml/1 tbsp icing (confectioners') sugar
½ cantaloupe melon

1 Preheat the grill (broiler) to high. Hull the strawberries and cut them in half.

2 Arrange the strawberries in a single layer, cut-side up, on a baking sheet or in an ovenproof dish and dust them with the icing sugar.

3 Grill (broil) the strawberries for 4–5 minutes, or until the sugar starts to bubble and turn golden.

4 Meanwhile, scoop out the seeds from the half melon using a spoon. Using a sharp knife, remove the skin, then cut the flesh into wedges.

5 Arrange on a serving plate with the grilled strawberries. Serve immediately.

Variation

Use fragrant, orange-fleshed Charentais melon instead of cantaloupe melon.

Cook's Tip

Fragrant, orange-fleshed varieties of melon, such as cantaloupe and Charentais, have a higher vitamin-C content than Watermelons. Avoid buying them ready-cut because most of the vitamins will have been lost.

Melon Trio with Ginger Cookies

The eye-catching colours of these three different melons really make this dessert, while the crisp biscuits provide a perfect contrast in terms of texture.

Serves 4

¼ watermelon
½ honeydew melon
½ Charentais melon
60ml/4 tbsp stem ginger syrup

For the cookies

25g/1oz/2 tbsp unsalted butter
25g/1oz/2 tbsp caster (superfine) sugar
5ml/1 tsp clear honey
25g/1oz/¼ cup plain (all-purpose) flour
25g/1oz/¼ cup luxury glacé mixed fruit, finely chopped
1 1.5cm/½in piece of preserved stem ginger in syrup, drained and finely chopped
30ml/2 tbsp flaked almonds

1 Remove the seeds from the melons, then cut them into wedges and slice off the rind. Cut all the flesh into chunks and mix in a bowl. Stir in the stem ginger syrup, cover and chill until ready to serve.

2 Meanwhile, make the cookies. Preheat the oven to 180°C/350°F/Gas 4. Place the butter, sugar and honey in a pan and heat until melted. Remove from the heat and stir in the remaining ingredients.

3 Line a baking sheet with baking parchment. Space four spoonfuls of the mixture on the paper at regular intervals, leaving plenty of room to allow for the cookies spreading. Flatten the mixture slightly into rounds and bake for 15 minutes or until the tops are golden.

4 Let the cookies cool on the baking sheet for 1 minute, then lift each one in turn, using a metal spatula, and drape over a rolling pin to cool and harden. Repeat with the remaining ginger mixture to make eight curved cookies in all.

5 Transfer the melon chunks and syrup to a large serving dish or individual glasses and serve accompanied by the crisp ginger cookies.

Cantaloupe melon with strawberries: Energy 53kcal/223kJ; Protein 0.9g; Carbohydrate 12.7g, of which sugars 12.7g; Fat 0.2g, of which saturates 0g; Cholesterol 0mg; Calcium 23mg; Fibre 0.8g; Sodium 41mg
Melon trio with ginger cookies: Energy 350kcal/1479kJ; Protein 4.8g; Carbohydrate 65g, of which sugars 60.1g; Fat 9.7g, of which saturates 3.8g; Cholesterol 13mg; Calcium 74mg; Fibre 2.5g; Sodium 167mg

Grilled Pineapple with Papaya Sauce

Pineapple cooked this way takes on a superb flavour and is quite sensational when served with the papaya sauce.

Serves 6
1 sweet pineapple
melted butter, for greasing and brushing
2 pieces drained preserved stem ginger in syrup, cut into fine matchsticks, plus 30ml/2 tbsp of the syrup from the jar
30ml/2 tbsp demerara (raw) sugar
pinch of ground cinnamon
fresh mint sprigs, to decorate

For the sauce
1 ripe papaya, peeled and seeded
175ml/6fl oz/¾ cup apple juice

1 Peel the pineapple and take spiral slices off the outside to remove the eyes. Cut the pineapple crossways into six slices, each 2.5cm/1in thick.

2 Line a baking sheet with a sheet of foil, rolling up the sides to make a rim. Grease the foil with some melted butter. Preheat the grill (broiler).

3 Arrange the pineapple slices on the lined baking sheet. Brush with butter, then top with the ginger matchsticks, sugar and cinnamon. Drizzle over the stem ginger syrup. Grill (broil) for 5–7 minutes or until the slices are golden and lightly charred.

4 Meanwhile, to make the sauce, cut a few slices from the papaya and set aside, then purée the rest with the apple juice in a blender or food processor.

5 Press the purée through a sieve (strainer) placed over a bowl, then stir in any juices from cooking the pineapple.

6 Serve the pineapple slices with sauce drizzled around each plate. Decorate with the reserved papaya slices and the mint sprigs.

Tropical Fruit Gratin

This out-of-the-ordinary gratin is strictly for grown-ups. A colourful combination of fruit is topped with a simple sabayon before being flashed under the grill.

Serves 4
2 tamarillos
½ sweet pineapple
1 ripe mango
175g/6oz/1½ cups blackberries
120ml/4fl oz/½ cup sparkling white wine
115g/4oz/½ cup caster (superfine) sugar
6 egg yolks

1 Cut each tamarillo in half lengthwise and then into thick slices. Cut the rind and core from the pineapple and take spiral slices off the outside to remove the eyes. Cut the flesh into regular chunks. Peel the mango, cut it in half and slice the flesh from the stone.

2 Divide all the fruit, including the blackberries, among four 14cm/5½in gratin dishes set on a baking sheet and set aside. Heat the wine and sugar in a pan until the sugar has dissolved. Bring to the boil and cook for 5 minutes.

3 Put the egg yolks in a large heatproof bowl. Place the bowl over a pan of simmering water and whisk until pale. Slowly pour on the hot sugar syrup, whisking all the time, until the mixture thickens. Preheat the grill (broiler).

4 Spoon the mixture over the fruit. Place the baking sheet holding the dishes on a low shelf under the hot grill until the topping is golden. Serve immediately.

Cook's Tip
Blackberries are widely cultivated from late spring to autumn and are usually large, plump and sweet. The finest wild blackberries have a bitter edge and a strong depth of flavour – best appreciated with a sprinkling of sugar.

Grilled pineapple with papaya: Energy 130kcal/558kJ; Protein 1g; Carbohydrate 32.9g, of which sugars 32.9g; Fat 0.4g, of which saturates 0g; Cholesterol 0mg; Calcium 49mg; Fibre 3.4g; Sodium 21mg
Tropical fruit gratin: Energy 300kcal/1270kJ; Protein 6.2g; Carbohydrate 52.8g, of which sugars 52.7g; Fat 8.7g, of which saturates 2.4g; Cholesterol 302mg; Calcium 119mg; Fibre 4.6g; Sodium 22mg

Banana & Mascarpone

If you are a fan of cold banana custard, you'll love this recipe. It is a grown-up version of an old favourite. No one will guess that the secret is ready-made custard sauce.

Serves 4–6
250g/9oz/generous 1 cup mascarpone cheese
300ml/½ pint/1¼ cups fresh ready-made custard sauce
150ml/¼ pint/⅔ cup Greek (US strained plain) yogurt
4 bananas
juice of 1 lime
50g/2oz/½ cup pecan nuts, coarsely chopped
120ml/4fl oz/½ cup maple syrup

1 Combine the mascarpone, custard sauce and yogurt in a large bowl and beat together until smooth. Make this mixture up to several hours ahead, if you like. Cover and chill, then stir before using.

2 Slice the bananas diagonally and place in a separate bowl. Pour over the lime juice and toss together until the bananas are coated in the juice.

3 Divide half the custard mixture between four to six dessert glasses and top each portion with a generous spoonful of the banana mixture.

4 Spoon the remaining custard mixture into the glasses and top with the rest of the bananas. Scatter the nuts over the top. Drizzle maple syrup over each dessert and chill for 30 minutes before serving.

Cook's Tips
- *Fresh custard sauce is now readily available from the chilled sections of supermarkets. Canned can be used if necessary.*
- *If pecans are not available, use roughly chopped toasted walnuts or flaked (sliced) almonds.*

Strawberries in a Raspberry & Passion Fruit Sauce

Fragrant strawberries release their finest flavour when moistened with a sauce of fresh raspberries and scented passion fruit.

Serves 4
350g/12oz/2 cups raspberries, fresh or frozen
45ml/3 tbsp caster (superfine) sugar
1 passion fruit
675g/1½lb/6 cups small strawberries
8 plain finger biscuits, to serve

1 Place the raspberries and sugar in a stain-resistant pan and soften over a gentle heat to release the juices. Simmer gently for 5 minutes. Allow to cool.

2 Halve the passion fruit and, using a teaspoon, carefully scoop out the seeds and juice.

3 Turn the raspberries into a food processor or blender, add the passion fruit and blend until well combined.

4 Pass the blended fruit sauce through a fine nylon sieve (strainer) to remove the seeds.

5 Fold the strawberries into the sauce, then spoon into four stemmed glasses. Serve with plain finger biscuits.

Variation
You could try serving the strawberries with an uncooked raspberry purée or coulis instead. Place some raspberries, with lemon juice and icing (confectioners') sugar to taste, in a food processor or blender and process until smooth. Press through a nylon sieve (strainer) to remove the seeds. You can store the purée in the refrigerator for up to 2 days.

Banana & mascarpone: Energy 222kcal/931kJ; Protein 5.6g; Carbohydrate 27.8g, of which sugars 25.5g; Fat 10.4g, of which saturates 3.8g; Cholesterol 12mg; Calcium 64mg; Fibre 0.8g; Sodium 62mg
Strawberries in raspberry sauce: Energy 113kcal/481kJ; Protein 2.7g; Carbohydrate 26.1g, of which sugars 26.1g; Fat 0.5g, of which saturates 0.1g; Cholesterol 0mg; Calcium 55mg; Fibre 4.2g; Sodium 14mg

Mixed Melon Salad with Wild Strawberries

Ice-cold melon is a delicious way to end a meal. Here, several varieties are combined with strongly flavoured wild or woodland strawberries.

Serves 4
1 cantaloupe or Charentais melon
1 Galia melon
900g/2lb watermelon
175g/6oz/1 ½ cups wild strawberries
4 fresh mint sprigs, to decorate

1 Using a large, sharp knife, cut all the melons in half. Remove the seeds from the halved cantaloupe and Galia melons using a spoon.

2 With a melon baller, scoop out as many melon balls as you can from all three melons.

3 Transfer to a large bowl, mix gently together and chill.

4 Add the wild strawberries and turn out into four stemmed glass dishes.

5 Decorate with sprigs of fresh mint and serve.

Cook's Tips
• *If the tiny wild strawberries are not available, you can use ordinary strawberries instead. Just cut them in half before adding them.*
• *Mix the fruits together gently as they will break up and damage easily.*
• *Strawberries are rich in B complex vitamins and vitamin C. They contain significant amounts of potassium and have good skin-cleansing properties.*
• *Store strawberries in the refrigerator and eat on day of purchase.*

Muscat Grape Frappé

The flavour and perfume of the Muscat grape is wonderful in this ice-cool, sophisticated salad.

Serves 4
½ bottle Muscat wine
150ml/¼ pint/⅔ cup water
450g/1lb Muscat grapes

1 Pour the wine into a stainless-steel or enamel tray, add the water, place in the freezer and freeze for 3 hours, until solid.

2 Remove the seeds from the grapes with a pair of tweezers. If you have time, you can also peel the grapes. Scrape across the frozen wine with a tablespoon to make a fine ice. Combine the grapes with the ice, spoon into four shallow glasses and serve.

Apricots in Marsala

Apricots gently poached in Marsala and served chilled make a versatile dessert. Serve with sweetened whipped cream mixed with yogurt and flavoured with ground cinnamon.

Serves 4
12 apricots
50g/2oz/4tbsp caster (superfine) sugar
300ml/½ pint/1 ¼ cups Marsala
2 strips pared orange rind
1 vanilla pod (bean), split
250ml/8fl oz/1 cup water

1 Halve and stone (pit) the apricots, then place in a bowl of boiling water for about 30 seconds. Drain, then slip off the skins.

2 Place the sugar, Marsala, orange rind, vanilla pod and water in a pan. Heat gently until the sugar dissolves. Bring to the boil, without stirring, then simmer for 2–3 minutes.

3 Add the apricot halves and poach for 5–6 minutes, or until just tender. Using a slotted spoon, transfer to a serving dish. Boil the syrup rapidly until reduced by half, then pour over the apricots and leave to cool. Cover and chill. Remove the orange rind and vanilla pod before serving.

Mixed melon salad: Energy 154kcal/655kJ; Protein 3g; Carbohydrate 35.4g, of which sugars 35.4g; Fat 1g, of which saturates 0.2g; Cholesterol 0mg; Calcium 62mg; Fibre 1.9g; Sodium 100mg
Muscat grape frappé: Energy 150kcal/634kJ; Protein 0.6g; Carbohydrate 22.5g, of which sugars 22.5g; Fat 0.1g, of which saturates 0g; Cholesterol 0mg; Calcium 27mg; Fibre 0.8g; Sodium 14mg
Apricots in Marsala: Energy 159kcal/673kJ; Protein 1.3g; Carbohydrate 26.5g, of which sugars 26.5g; Fat 0.1g, of which saturates 0g; Cholesterol 0mg; Calcium 36mg; Fibre 2.1g; Sodium 13mg

Fresh Fruit with Mango Sauce

Fruit coulis became trendy in the 1970s with nouvelle cuisine. It makes a simple fruit dish special.

Serves 6

1 large ripe mango, peeled, stoned (pitted) and chopped
rind of 1 unwaxed orange
juice of 3 oranges
caster (superfine) sugar, to taste
2 peaches
2 nectarines
1 small mango, peeled
2 plums
1 pear or ½ small melon
25–50g/1–2oz/2 heaped tbsp wild strawberries (optional)
25–50g/1–2oz/2 heaped tbsp raspberries
25–50g/1–2oz/2 heaped tbsp blueberries
juice of 1 lemon
small mint sprigs, to decorate

1 In a food processor fitted with the metal blade, process the large mango until smooth. Add the orange rind, juice and sugar to taste and process again until very smooth. Press through a sieve (strainer) into a bowl and chill the sauce.

2 Peel the peaches, if you like, then slice and stone (pit) the peaches, nectarines, small mango and plums. Quarter and core the pear, or if using, slice the melon thinly and remove the peel.

3 Place the sliced fruits on a large plate, sprinkle the fruits with the lemon juice and chill, covered with clear film (plastic wrap), for up to 3 hours before serving.

4 To serve, arrange the sliced fruits on serving plates, spoon the berries on top, drizzle with a little mango sauce and decorate with mint sprigs. Serve the remaining sauce separately.

Variation

Use a raspberry coulis instead of a mango one: purée raspberries with a little lemon juice and icing (confectioners') sugar to taste, then pass through a sieve (strainer) to remove the pips. You can use frozen raspberries for this, so it can be made at any time of year.

Bananas with Lime & Cardamom Sauce

Cardamom and bananas go together perfectly, and this luxurious dessert makes a really original treat. Vanilla or coconut ice cream makes a fabulous accompaniment.

Serves 4

6 small bananas
50g/2oz/¼ cup butter
seeds from 4 cardamom pods, crushed
50g/2oz/½ cup flaked (sliced) almonds
thinly pared rind and juice of 2 limes
50g/2oz/⅓ cup light muscovado (brown) sugar
30ml/2 tbsp dark rum
ice cream, to serve

1 Peel the bananas and cut them in half lengthwise. Heat half the butter in a large frying pan. Add half the bananas, and cook until the undersides are golden. Turn carefully, using a metal spatula. Cook until golden all over.

2 Once cooked, transfer the bananas to a heatproof serving dish. Cook the remaining bananas in the same way.

3 Melt the remaining butter, then add the cardamom seeds and almonds. Cook, stirring until the almonds are golden.

4 Stir in the lime rind and juice, then the sugar. Cook, stirring, until the mixture is smooth, bubbling and slightly reduced. Stir in the rum. Pour the sauce over the bananas and serve with ice cream.

Cook's Tip

Use green cardamom pods. Split them open and scrape out the black seeds, then crush to help release the aromatic flavour.

Variation

If serving to children, replace the rum with orange juice.

Fresh fruit with mango sauce: Energy 82kcal/351kJ; Protein 1.9g; Carbohydrate 19.2g, of which sugars 19.1g; Fat 0.3g, of which saturates 0.1g; Cholesterol 0mg; Calcium 22mg; Fibre 3.3g; Sodium 5mg
Bananas with lime & cardamom: Energy 350kcal/1462kJ; Protein 4.2g; Carbohydrate 41.9g, of which sugars 38.8g; Fat 17.6g, of which saturates 7.2g; Cholesterol 27mg; Calcium 46mg; Fibre 2.3g; Sodium 80mg

Indian Fruit Salad

This lightly spiced salad is ideal after a heavy meal.

Serves 6

115g/4oz seedless green and black grapes
225g/8oz canned mandarin segments, drained
2 navel oranges, peeled and segmented
225g/8oz canned grapefruit segments, drained
1 honeydew melon and ½ watermelon, flesh cut into balls
1 fresh mango, peeled, stoned (pitted) and sliced
juice of 1 lemon
2.5ml/½ tsp sugar
1.5ml/¼ tsp ground cumin seeds
salt and ground black pepper

1 Place all the fruit in a large serving bowl and add the lemon juice. Gently toss to prevent damaging the fruit.

2 Mix together the remaining ingredients and sprinkle over the fruit. Gently toss, chill thoroughly and serve.

Chinese Fruit Salad

An unusual fruit salad with an Oriental flavour, ideal for rounding off a spicy meal.

Serves 4

115g/4oz/½ cup caster (superfine) sugar
300ml/½ pint/1¼ cups water
thinly pared rind and juice of 1 lime
400g/14oz can lychees in syrup
1 ripe mango, peeled and sliced
1 eating apple, cored and sliced
2 bananas, chopped
1 star fruit, sliced (optional)
5ml/1 tsp sesame seeds, toasted

1 Place the sugar in a pan with the water and the lime rind. Heat gently until the sugar dissolves, then increase the heat and boil gently for about 7–8 minutes. Set aside to cool.

2 Drain the lychees and reserve the juice. Pour the juice into the cooled lime syrup with the lime juice. Place all the prepared fruit in a bowl and pour on the lime and lychee syrup. Chill for about 1 hour. Just before serving, sprinkle with sesame seeds.

Papayas in Tropical Jasmine Flower Syrup

The fragrant syrup can be prepared in advance, using fresh jasmine flowers from a house plant or the garden. It tastes fabulous with papayas, but it is also good with other tropical fruits, such as lychees or mangoes.

Serves 2

105ml/7 tbsp water
45ml/3 tbsp palm sugar (jaggery) or light muscovado (brown) sugar
20–30 jasmine flowers, plus a few extra, to decorate (optional)
2 ripe papayas
juice of 1 lime

1 Place the water and sugar in a small pan. Heat gently, stirring occasionally, until the sugar has dissolved, then simmer, without stirring, over a low heat for 4 minutes.

2 Pour into a bowl, leave to cool slightly, then add the jasmine flowers. Leave to steep for at least 20 minutes.

3 Peel the papayas and slice in half lengthwise. Scoop out and discard the seeds. Plate the papayas and squeeze lime over.

4 Strain the syrup into a clean bowl, discarding the flowers. Spoon the syrup over the papayas. Serve at once, decorated with a few fresh jasmine flowers.

Cook's Tip
Although scented white jasmine flowers are perfectly safe to eat, be sure that they have not been sprayed with pesticides or other harmful chemicals. Washing them may not remove all the residue.

Variation
Spoon the warm syrup over a tall glass of ice cream to create a quick but stylish dessert.

Indian fruit salad: Energy 120kcal/512kJ; Protein 2.6g; Carbohydrate 28.6g, of which sugars 28.5g; Fat 0.3g, of which saturates 0g; Cholesterol 0mg; Calcium 67mg; Fibre 3.5g; Sodium 61mg
Chinese fruit salad: Energy 264kcal/1123kJ; Protein 1.7g; Carbohydrate 66.1g, of which sugars 64.9g; Fat 1g, of which saturates 0.2g; Cholesterol 0mg; Calcium 36mg; Fibre 2.4g; Sodium 6mg
Papayas in jasmine flower syrup: Energy 197kcal/837kJ; Protein 1.6g; Carbohydrate 49.9g, of which sugars 49.9g; Fat 0.3g, of which saturates 0g; Cholesterol 0mg; Calcium 81mg; Fibre 6.6g; Sodium 17mg

Index